51-12

Hamlet's Fictions

Hamlet's Fictions

—

MAURICE CHARNEY

ROUTLEDGE
New York and London

First published in 1988 by
Routledge, Chapman and Hall
29 West 35th Street, New York NY 10001

Published in Great Britain by
Routledge
11 New Fetter Lane, London EC4P 4EE

Typeset by AKM Associates (UK) Ltd, London
Printed in Great Britain at the
University Printing House, Cambridge

Library of Congress Cataloging in Publication Data

Charney, Maurice
  Hamlet's fictions / Maurice Charney.
  p.   cm.
  Bibliogrphy: p.
  Includes index.
  ISBN 0-415-00703-8
  1. Shakespeare, William, 1564–1616.   Hamlet.   I. Title.
PR2807.C278 1988
822.3′3——dc19

British Library Cataloguing in Publication Data
Charney, Maurice
  Hamlet's fictions.
  1. Shakespeare, William.   Hamlet
  I. Title
  822.3′3   PR2807
  ISBN 415-00703-8

To the memory of
all those good and lovable people
who are no longer with us:
BENJAMIN and SADIE CHARNEY, FRIDA KURZ,
LAJOS and POLDI WOLF,
ARTIE WIENER, JULIAN KAYE,
and BERNIE BECKERMAN

Contents

Preface

Hamlet's Fictions is, in some sense, a sequel to *Style in "Hamlet,"* published by Princeton University Press in 1969. Both books focus strongly on matters of imagery and style, but *Hamlet's Fictions* develops new topics related to image-making, fantasy, and the trying out of fictions by characters on their own behalf and on behalf of the play. *Hamlet* as a work of the theatrical imagination seems to me now more complex and more impenetrable than it did in 1969, but it is also a simple and powerful narrative. The purpose of another book is to explore this paradox. *Hamlet* is strikingly original. It is a revenge play with a difference. Although it is strongly grounded in the popular dramatic tradition, it is unusual in its intellectuality and its constant play of speculation and displacement. What I have called "fictions" is called by other names by other critics, but we are all trying to speak about the special creativity of the play.

Shakespeare is quoted throughout from the single volumes of the Signet edition, under the general editorship of Sylvan Barnet. *Hamlet* is edited by Edward Hubler (in 1963), and it relies heavily on the Quarto 2 edition. The Signet Shakespeare has been conveniently collected into a single volume published by Harcourt, Brace, Jovanovich in 1972. Dates of Elizabethan and Jacobean plays are given from Alfred Harbage, *Annals of English Drama 975-1700*, rev. S. Schoenbaum, London, 1964.

I am grateful to the editors of *Mosaic, Signs, Shakespeare Bulletin, Renaissance Drama*, and *Modern Drama* for allowing me to reprint materials, in a revised form, that originally appeared in their pages. I am also grateful to the Editor of Fairleigh Dickinson

University Press for permitting me to use, in a revised form, an essay that appeared in *Psychoanalytic Approaches to Literature and Film*, edited by Maurice Charney and Joseph Reppen, 1987, and to the editor of University of Delaware Press for an essay in *Shakespeare and the Sense of Performance*, edited by Marvin and Ruth Thompson, 1988. Thanks are also due to the Research Council of Rutgers University and its learned staff, especially Fred Main, for support of this project at various stages. I got a lot of help very early in my enterprise from my graduate assistant, Ray Klimek.

But in a fiction, in a dream of passion . . .

Introduction

Starting from the assumption that we all know Shakespeare and that his language has been absorbed into our discourse, how can we recreate *Hamlet* "when new," to borrow a phrase from William Empson?[1] Can you imagine being in the audience when the word "heartache" was used for the first time in its modern sense of spiritual perturbation: "and by a sleep to say we end / The heartache, and the thousand natural shocks / That flesh is heir to" (3.1.61–63)? This is a great moment in the history of the English language. As readers, primarily, of Shakespeare, we need to mediate between the printed page and our limited experience as spectators. The basic question is: how can we recreate the life of the spoken and acted language of the plays? If we cannot literally recover *Hamlet* "when new," we can at least try to understand the symbolic and theatrical context of the play that Shakespeare wrote and presented around the beginning of the seventeenth century.

There may have been some literal vitality in the lines, some special appropriateness in the theatrical situation that we are now missing. These are not learned allusions, but bits and pieces of ordinary experience that need to be revivified. In the shortened version of *King Lear* by the late Buzz Goodbody (and the Royal Shakespeare Company) presented in 1974 at the Brooklyn Academy of Music, I was suddenly struck by a line to which I hadn't paid any attention, Gloucester's woeful sense of Lear's predicament on the heath: "For many miles about / There's scarce a bush" (2.4.300–1). Goneril and Regan and Cornwall are determined that Gloucester must shut up his doors and that the willful Lear must be taught a lesson by this wild night. Until his blinding, Gloucester is an expert in the ineffectual protest, and his querulousness has been well understood by the theatrical tradition. But there is a special poignancy in his glimmerings of insight:

> Alack, the night comes on, and the high winds
> Do sorely ruffle. For many miles about
> There's scarce a bush.   (2.4.299–301)

Without making any metadramatic claims for Shakespeare, I think these lines may have a unique application to Brooklyn, especially the bombed-out, urban renewal area that surrounds the Brooklyn Academy near Flatbush Avenue (but Flatbush itself is many miles away). "Scarce a bush" suggests a nature so minimal that even a bush would contradict its barrenness. We seem to be metaphorically well above the tree line. *King Lear* depends upon our symbolic equation of the inner and outer nature – nature physical and moral – yet we still need to apprehend literally the sinking barrenness of "scarce a bush" before we can appreciate the moral desolation. This is not a dead metaphor, and the perspective is large: "For *many* miles about." Nature is participating in Lear's divestiture. The theatrical situation is designed to represent pathetic fallacy.

This not very remarkable line from *King Lear* sparks an unpredictable vitality in the presented play that has nothing to do with the formal eloquence of set speeches.[2] The theatrical tide has turned against the big speeches in Shakespeare, especially the long soliloquies, perhaps because they attempt large emotional effects that are difficult to bring off. In Joe Papp's parody *Hamlet* (now known as "Naked *Hamlet*"[3]), an early offering at the Public Theater in New York, the "To be, or not to be" soliloquy was spoken in a histrionic Puerto Rican accent, while Hamlet, with his feet dangling from the upper stage, cracked peanuts and threw the shells at the audience. The embarrassment with eloquence derives from a feeling that the eloquent parts of Shakespeare are those that readers already know too well – perhaps even know by heart from an early school assignment – so that it is up to the director to mount a production that is not merely another reading of an already well-read play. This is the revolt against classic, schoolboy

Shakespeare, and it is sometimes carried to such absurd lengths that mere novelty replaces any interpretation at all, and the play we know and cherish disappears into some grotesque directorial simulacrum. Obviously, verbal eloquence is not enough in itself to carry a play – a notion based on older, rhetorical ideas found in Cicero and Quintilian that insist that the play is a form of oratory.

The problem is that Shakespeare has become a cultural palimpsest, and we need to proceed layer by underlying layer to recover, as Schliemann did with Troy (or thought he did), the basic substratum. We return to the naive question of what a Shakespearean play must have seemed like to its first audiences.[4] Or, to narrow the topic, can we speak, in Empson's terms, of *Hamlet* "when new"? Empson saw the real *Hamlet* problem as one experienced by the play's first audiences. I am convinced that the play must have come across as an exciting and very original revenge action, and not at all a contemplative drama of a man who could not make up his mind (as in the romantic Olivier film). The revenge-play conventions were still fresh in people's under-standing, conventions that could be invoked automatically and spontaneously and without the fatal touch of artifice – the way we instinctively understand the rules of science fiction, spy movies, and TV sitcoms.

Hamlet "when new" must have reminded spectators of *The Spanish Tragedy*, which may have been the most popular play of its time. It is certainly the most parodied. It is logical to assume that if Shakespeare had an immediate source for *Hamlet* it could well have been an earlier version of the Hamlet story by Thomas Kyd, author of *The Spanish Tragedy*, or by one of the University Wits. We know nothing directly about this earlier version, called without much attempt at verisimilitude the *Ur-Hamlet*, but its Ghost seems to have made a strong impression. In Thomas Lodge's allusion, the Ghost "cried so miserably at the Theater, like an oyster wife, 'Hamlet, revenge.' "[5] Is this the first Elizabethan public playhouse, The Theater, which was built by the Burbages in 1579? The allusion in the Induction to *A Warning for Fair Women* (c. 1599) may or may not refer to the *Ur-Hamlet*, but it is worth quoting for its own strong passions:

> a filthy whining ghost,
> Lapped in some foul sheet, or a leather pilch,
> Come screaming like a pig half-stickt,
> And cries, "Vindicta, revenge, revenge...."[6]

"Like a pig half-stickt" is a vivid reminder of the bloodiness expected from a revenge action.

The bloodiness of Shakespeare's *Hamlet*? This is an aspect of the play we prefer to ignore, as if it were necessary for Shakespeare to kosher the bleeding carcass of the *Ur-Hamlet* before he could present it at our more civilized table. I am not going to proceed any further with this conjecture about the mythical *Ur-Hamlet* (usually asterisked by older and more exact critics to indicate its hypothetical status). If *Hamlet* is a cultural palimpsest, we are still deeply buried in Romantic strata of the play. We don't want our hero to be cruel, bloody, and unnatural, even when Shakespeare is at great pains to tell us that he is. We ignore an aspect of the play that seems obvious to me and to other readers of Elizabethan revenge tragedy: that Hamlet is a revenger, who, in actively pursuing his revenge, becomes tainted (and therefore tragically doomed) by his involvement in the process of revenge.

The decline of *Hamlet* in our time should not surprise us. As L. C. Knights puts it, "in the twentieth century, *Hamlet* has yielded to *King Lear* the distinction of being the play in which the age most finds itself."[7] We feel the pathos of *Lear* as a family tragedy, the intensity of its suffering, and the archetypal quality of its passion. King Lear rages for all of us against the gods. But in *Hamlet* the tragedy seems unacceptably crude, especially in the areas of sex and death, and its status as a revenge play makes it almost at once hostile to humanist ideologies. An important group of British critics, especially of the 1930s and 1940s, have inveighed against *Hamlet*'s harshness: among the more distinguished are L. C. Knights, G. Wilson Knight, T. S. Eliot, Derek Traversi, and other critics associated with F. R. Leavis and *Scrutiny*. These critics more or less assume the inferiority of *Hamlet* as a tragedy, especially in ideological and ethical terms. Hamlet is immature and incapable of dealing with adult experience. He is violent – an especially grave fault – and unable to overcome his fascination with what he most condemns. Like the dyer's hand of Sonnet 111, Hamlet's nature "is subdued / To what it works in" and thereby suffers an ineradicable stain. These moral criteria are still operative in the more recent criticism of the play.

As a representative sample of the attack on *Hamlet*, L. C. Knights's essay, "Prince Hamlet" (*Scrutiny*, 1940), states the case more directly and more baldly than his later modifications and expansions. Despite the many aspects of the play that he admires, Knights finds Hamlet essentially self-indulgent, immature, brutal, and self-righteous, and "The desire to escape from the complexities of adult living is central to Hamlet's character."[8] What "the complexities of adult living" are that Hamlet avoids is never explained, and it is assumed that all right-thinking persons will know what Knights is talking about. Hamlet suffers from "moral relaxation" rather than the intentness of moral scrutiny that Knights admires. Hamlet's wit is "entirely destructive, malicious and sterile."[9] Knights cannot forgive Hamlet his preoccupation with sex in relation both to Gertrude and to Ophelia, and this sexual nausea is clearly linked with Hamlet's preoccupation with death. This is precisely the theme of G. Wilson Knight's essay, "The Embassy of Death," in *The Wheel of Fire*, which dates from 1930. Knight berates Hamlet for his preoccupation with hate and death and comes to the astonishing conclusion that Claudius the murderer is an altogether more admirable and more attractive figure than the hating and death-fixated Hamlet.

In *An Approach to "Hamlet"* (1961), Knights develops his thesis with greater fullness and with a sustained comparison to other Shakespearean tragedies. The point of view, however, is quite similar to Knights's earlier *Scrutiny* essay. He cannot accept Hamlet's irresolution and his fascination with the evil he is supposed to condemn. Hamlet's passion and Hamlet's madness are both improper because they have no clear moral direction, and Knights would like to ignore Hamlet's fiction-making on which the present study is based. To Knights, Hamlet's involvement in play-acting and the histrionic shows only a lack of sincerity and an inability to think effectively. If Hamlet is an intellectual at all, he is a negative intellectual who is not an appropriate guide for the perplexed. He is inadequate in dealing with his own problems or in showing us how his problems can be conceptualized. In the most general sense, Hamlet is not up to the mark:

> with whatever excitements of his reason and his blood, [he] is a man who has given himself over to a false direction of consciousness; and at each of the crucial points of the action Shakespeare leaves us in no doubt of the inadequacy – and worse – of Hamlet's basic attitudes.[10]

As P. R. Grover points out, Knights's antipathy to *Hamlet* in some sense expresses a general dislike for Shakespearean tragedy, or at least of those areas of tragedy in which *Hamlet* does not resemble *King Lear*. Knights seems intent, according to Grover, "on taking the tragic out of tragedy,"[11] and he gives us a version of Shakespeare as Henry James might have written it, in which Hamlet should definitely not take revenge and not kill Claudius. The harshness and insolubility of the play, its preoccupation with sex and death, its insistence on revenge and murder even of the mostly innocent, its madness and histrionic posturing all offend Knights and other *Scrutiny* critics. As Kenneth Muir says of Knights, his is "the interpretation of a sensitive Scrutineer with a highly developed moral sense and, one suspects, with a distaste for the theater to which Shakespeare's plays really belong."[12] This is a crucial point that separates the criticism of Knights from later, theater-oriented and myth-directed critics.

The *Scrutiny* approach to *Hamlet* is already present in a review by T. S. Eliot in 1919, centering on J. M. Robertson's disintegrationist theories of the play – theories that have long since been discarded. Eliot strongly argues the impropriety of the play, its inability to establish an "objective correlative" for the emotions it wishes to generate. "Hamlet (the man) is dominated by an emotion which is inexpressible, because it is in *excess* of the facts as they appear."[13] What Eliot means exactly has been much debated, but he clearly indicates that Hamlet's relation to his mother is problematic. The Gertrude of the play does not offer, in artistic terms, "an adequate equivalent" for the disgust Hamlet feels. In theatrical terms, Eliot seems to be saying that Hamlet's disgust is not properly motivated. Hamlet's wild imagination and histrionic frenzy are out of control; they are narcissistic rather than an expression of emotions directed to other characters. In order to argue with this specious proposition, one must also wrestle with Eliot's conviction that *Hamlet* is an artistic failure because Shakespeare was not up to the task he set himself, that he "tackled a problem which proved too much for him."[14] According to Eliot, *Hamlet* does not rightly belong with A. C. Bradley's four "great" tragedies of Shakespeare, but is instead a problem play which contains issues that have not been successfully developed. Its ambitions exceed its accomplishments.

In arguing for the validity of *Hamlet's* fictions my point is that the play has a wider imaginative thrust than Knights, Knight, and Eliot will allow. It extends the idea of tragedy beyond simple humanist convictions and ethical beliefs. The revenge play as a genre forces us to look beyond our neat formulas based on Aristotle's *Poetics* and to abandon ethical abstractions that have little relation to the possibilities of ordinary experience. As a tragedy *Hamlet* makes greater demands on our sensibilities than *King Lear* and *Othello* in the sense that we are much less prepared by our training and education for what *Hamlet* is about. We are much less able to accept the world of *Hamlet* and its assumptions about the nature of things. *Macbeth* seems to me much closer to *Hamlet* in this respect because it too is a play about murder and its consequences. Our Aristotelian ideas of tragedy are not well adapted to murder and revenge, which makes understanding *Hamlet* difficult. Murder and revenge are too primitive and too powerful anthropologically to be judged by our limited ethical criteria.

Hamlet's Fictions emphasizes the play as a fiction, a narrative, a series of wish-fulfillment projections in a story about murder and revenge. We are trying to find out what is preoccupying Hamlet and other characters and how their preoccupations create the dramatic action. It hardly needs repeating that the play itself is a fiction, in which the fictions of individual characters take their proper place. Hamlet is trying to make judgments about the world

around him, or the fragmentation of that world, in terms of what
he knows, what he sees, and what he desires. In some sense, he is
treating himself as a dramatic character thrust into a lurid story of
murder and revenge in which he is not entirely comfortable. As
much as he tries to slip out, he is sucked into the center of the
action by a centripetal force of consciousness. Like Oedipus, he
gradually becomes the tragic protagonist whether he wants to or
not; as he learns more about what has happened, he also becomes
more central to the sequence of events as they unfold. In other
words, his own pursuit of knowledge involves him in the tragic
scenario. By "fiction" I mean to identify a character's own
understanding of the narrative context of which he is a part and to
understand how he plans to deal with the crises and emergencies he
faces. His strategies are also his fictions in so far as they both
participate in the imagination of disaster.

The book is divided into three, semi-autonomous parts, each of
which expresses some aspect of *Hamlet's* fiction. Most immediate is
"Part One: Passion and its Fictions", which grows out of Hamlet's
statement, "But in a fiction, in a dream of passion" (2.2.562), a
disturbing preoccupation of the "rogue and peasant slave"
soliloquy. "What's Hecuba to him [the Player], or he to Hecuba, /
That he should weep for her?" (569–70) is at the heart of the
histrionic argument. If Hamlet could possibly understand that, he
could understand everything that is happening to him. The first
chapter, "Hamlet's dream of passion," takes up the centrality of
"passion" as a key word and key concept in the play, more than in
any other play of Shakespeare. Is Hamlet's passion real or feigned,
and in what sense does it differ from the passion of Laertes,
Pyrrhus, Fortinbras, and the First Player? Hamlet advises the
Players to control and moderate passion and not let all slip by
overacting, as the players do in *The Mousetrap*. Horatio, who is not
"passion's slave," is something of an ideal figure, yet Hamlet
cannot imitate his moderation and reasonableness. It is as if the
tragic choices deeply commit the protagonist to a passion he
cannot hope either to understand or to control.

Shakespeare's Pirandellism in *Hamlet* turns on the theme of
passion, which deeply concerned both playwrights. There is a

three-way link between Pirandello's *Six Characters*, Stoppard's *Rosencrantz and Guildenstern Are Dead*, and Shakespeare's *Hamlet*, insofar as all three revolve around the fictionality of passion. The dream of passion is in itself a fiction, no matter how histrionically justified it may seem, and the six characters' insistence that it is all real and all happening now is the ultimate illusion. But if it is only a fiction, how can we explain the terror of Stoppard's Rosencrantz and Guildenstern, who will soon be dead?

Two additional chapters round off the passion theme in *Hamlet*: "Ophelia and other madwomen in Elizabethan plays" and "Hamlet's O-groans and textual criticism." Madness is one outlet for passion both in Hamlet's feigned madness and in the very touching lunacy by which Ophelia suddenly achieves identity in the play. Ophelia is seen in relation to other madwomen in Elizabethan drama, many of whom imitate aspects of her role: she is irreverent, bawdy, threatening (especially in relation to her father's "maimèd rites"), and altogether lyrical and pathetic. She acts out a passion that was totally closed to her before. Hamlet's O-groans, which have disappeared from most editions of the play, also act out a passionate death speech that is distasteful to most critics, textual and otherwise. It is interesting how conventional these O-groans were to express passion, leaving the particular nuance of repeated "O's" to the actor. This chapter juxtaposes the demands of the spoken, histrionic play and the desire of editors to establish a more permanent and respectable text. O-groans are not very literary or quotable.

Our second large division deals with the organization and disposition of dramatic energies. In other words, how is the Hamlet fiction worked out in relation to beginning, middle, and end? How is the imagination of the play deployed in all of its significant parts? How is one aspect of the structure anticipated or projected onto another? *Hamlet* makes important use of analogy and infinite regress, which suggest a sideways movement of the action rather than a forward progression. Not delay but displacement lies at the heart of the fiction, as if it were only through infinite regress that Hamlet could satisfy his intense craving for contemplation rather than action. But the ending is finally produced by a leap out of the infinite regress system.

There is a strong emphasis on the middle of *Hamlet*, and it looks as if this aspect of the structure is established with unusual clarity. In this chapter we see Hamlet trying out fictions of the revenger in the style of Pyrrhus, who slays Priam in the Player's Speech, and also of Fortinbras and of Laertes. In the clash of mighty opposites, Hamlet is trying to imitate Claudius, the secret poisoner, whose subtle murder in the porches of the ear the Ghost has reported. But Hamlet is no match for his uncle, and the whole middle action of the play is curiously displaced onto Polonius; it culminates, in fact, with the murder of Polonius, which is produced with brutal casualness and more or less by accident. All of these deep plots and deeper imaginings — the fictions of revenge — lead nowhere and must eventually cede to the new role of Providence at the end of the play. The chapter on "Scene rows, broken scenes, and impacted scenes" is a more technical account of the organization of the play into units of action that may be called "scene rows." These are often broken into two or three parts, with impacted or bridge scenes in between to allow for gaps in the narration. The structural units correspond with fictional sequences that are set against each other, or are, characteristically, represented in significant pieces rather than fully, as they would be in a novel.

Part Three of *Hamlet's Fictions* concerns itself with conventions of staging, imagery, and genre. The notion of conventions is itself a fiction of what the audience will accept for its willing suspension of disbelief. Drama, especially, depends upon a well understood pattern of expectations by which playwright and audience alike are guided in their anticipated reactions. *Hamlet* is not a Noh-play, and the strident claims its conventions make on us must seem in many ways puzzling to a non-Western audience. What does the Ghost of Hamlet's father want from his recalcitrant son, and why is revenge itself such an ambiguous and morally enigmatic topic? Such highly conventional stage devices as aside, soliloquy, and offstage speech have a dramatic impact that is difficult to account for by narrative purpose alone. By some agreed-upon fiction, we have endowed non-dialogic speech with a special truth-function that the dialogue itself does not have. We postulate that the characters on stage are speaking directly to us. The asides in *Hamlet* are especially surprising in their attempt to make narrative points that are not necessarily carried in the dramatic action. The extremely important soliloquies in the play seem to function autonomously as a system of reflection that works against the public dialogue. Interior monologue constitutes an inner play that often obtrudes on the dialogue and may not be fully consistent with it.

A brief chapter on the imagery of skin disease and sealing raises the issue of why these odd images should be more important in *Hamlet* than in any other play of Shakespeare. What are the implicit fictions on which these imageries feed? Obviously, in a play much concerned with secrecy and concealment, the image of the hidden skin disease should be crucial. Disease in the body natural and the body politic is covert and hidden, but horrible nevertheless. The imposthume, the ulcer, the tetter, and the cancer all allow for false appearances, "Whiles rank corruption, mining all within, / Infects unseen" (3.4.149–50). Sealing involves us in acts to which we give our free consent, and it therefore points up what characters do of their own accord, whether they wish to acknowledge it or not. To see the play in terms of voluntaristic fantasies is to take literally what the characters tell us and to ignore the large area of fiction-making and illusion. Claudius is especially associated with the tyrant's will, however cunningly his motives are disguised.

Our final chapter takes up the large question of *Hamlet* as comedy, which is played out against the more obvious claims of *Hamlet* as tragedy. Here, too, Polonius assumes a role of crucial importance, as if he has taken over the role of Claudius in the tragedy. *Hamlet* as comedy is, in some sense, a fiction against which *Hamlet* as tragedy is counterpointed. With which genre are we more comfortable? As Susan Snyder has pointed out in *The Comic Matrix of Shakespeare's Tragedies*, this is a general problem in thinking about the tragedies, especially in plays such as *Hamlet, King Lear*, and *Romeo and Juliet*. We have drawn on six comic elements in *Hamlet* – irrelevance, satire, madness, aggression, exuberance and wish-fulfillment, and the mastery of anxiety – although there are undoubtedly many more. The very large role of comedy in the play makes our sense of tragedy more acute, or at least gives it some black comedy overtones. Meaninglessness and absurdity, as in the dialogues with Osric and the Gravedigger, are overcome by courage and moral determination. Hamlet's fiction is finally resolved by his ability to act decisively in his own behalf. More covertly, the final fiction is Hamlet's apprehension of death, so that his ability to take revenge is dependent on his readiness to die.

PASSION AND ITS FICTIONS

1

Hamlet's dream of passion

It is significant that "passion" should be such a key word and key image in *Hamlet*. It is used more frequently in this play than anywhere else in the canon, and its thirteen examples suggest some covert revelations. In Elizabethan English the passions are the emotions, and Onions in *A Shakespeare Glossary* (based on the *OED*) defines the word as "applied widely to all kinds of feeling by which the mind is powerfully moved."[1] In the contemporary argument about the Stoics, moralists and theologians objected to Stoic doctrine because it so rigorously excluded the passions, which move men to good and evil. At the beginning of *The Taming of the Shrew*, Lucentio's servant, Tranio declares: "Let's be no stoics nor no stocks, I pray" (1.1.31). Since the passions apply particularly to love, the implication is that if you are not a Stoic, Ovid and his *Art of Love* will not "be an outcast quite abjured" (1.1.33). The neo-platonic ladder of love, as in Ficino, depends very strongly on the passions to lead one upward to spiritual states. Passion is necessary as a motive force for action. Without it we would be bland and passive, perhaps even totally rational, but hardly alive.

Most of the examples of "passion" in *Hamlet* occur in theatrical contexts, especially in two scenes relating to performance. There are four references in the Players' Scene (II,ii) and six more in the Play-Within-the-Play Scene (III,ii). "Passion" is a term more at home for Shakespeare in the theater than in life, so that it looks as if Hamlet needs to understand passion and make his peace with it before he can take revenge. The histrionic point is well demonstrated by Stoppard in *Rosencrantz and Guildenstern Are Dead*. His professional actors are at the center of the appearance-reality

conflict, and they baffle poor Rosencrantz and Guildenstern by
their ontological presence: they never enter but are always "On,"
and, of course, they never need to get into costumes to play their
roles. They are always ready.

Hamlet's first, very familiar conversation with the traveling
actors who visit Elsinore is to ask for a sample of their art: "We'll
have a speech straight. Come, give us a taste of your quality.
Come, a passionate speech" (2.2.440–42). Why a passionate
speech? Hamlet is already experimenting with the notion that
theater and life are in some ways indistinguishable. He takes
seriously the idea of the play as mimesis, an imitation of real life:

> I have heard that guilty creatures sitting at a play
> Have by the very cunning of the scene
> Been struck so to the soul that presently
> They have proclaimed their malefactions.
>
> (2.2.601–4)

In other words, murder will out; voluntarily or involuntarily,
there is no way of blocking it.

Hamlet is thinking of a specific passionate speech from a Dido
and Aeneas play (like Marlowe's *Dido Queen of Carthage* 1585–86?),
especially Aeneas' tale to Dido when he speaks of Priam's
slaughter. As a demonstration of passion, Hamlet recites thirteen
lines of a speech which seems to us highly rhetorical, formal, and
decoratively violent. The figure of Pyrrhus, looking for old Priam
in order to slay him, is not natural at all but superhuman,
overwrought, exaggeratedly dire and heroic:

> Roasted in wrath and fire,
> And thus o'ersizèd with coagulate gore,
> With eyes like carbuncles, the hellish Pyrrhus
> Old grandsire Priam seeks.   (2.2.472–75)

The grand passion of this passionate speech was beautifully
rendered in Kozintsev's *Hamlet* film,[2] where formality and
heightened rhetoric were stressed.

The First Player then takes up the Pyrrhus speech on Hamlet's
command: "So, proceed you" (2.2.476). The speech is an exercise

in declamatory passion, which concludes with an eloquent reference to "passion in the gods." When they heard "The instant burst of clamor" that Hecuba made when she saw "Pyrrhus make malicious sport / In mincing with his sword her husband's limbs," even the gods, who can feel no human sorrow, would have wept tears ("made milch the burning eyes of heaven") and felt an unaccustomed grief ("And passion in the gods") (524–29). This is "passion" in its primary sense of suffering, as in the Passion of Christ on the Cross. It is a hypothetical postulation of passion like Ariel's advice to Prospero about the compassion a spirit of the air might feel if it were human.

At this point the Player, like Hecuba, becomes passionate himself, turns "his color" and "has tears in's eyes" (530–31) and must break off his speech. This is what troubles Hamlet so profoundly in his soliloquy, that the Player, "But in a fiction, in a dream of passion" (562), could produce such powerful emotional effects:

> Could force his soul so to his own conceit
> That from her working all his visage wanned,
> Tears in his eyes, distraction in his aspect,
> A broken voice, and his whole function suiting
> With forms to his conceit?   (2.2.563–67)

The fictionality and the dream of passion in the Player baffle Hamlet, who cannot grasp where real life ends and theater begins. Why is the Player's weeping for Hecuba so futile, "all for nothing" (567)? "What's Hecuba to him, or he to Hecuba, / That he should weep for her?" (569–70).

But Hecuba exists only in relation to the Player's "passionate speech." Hecuba marks the "taste" of the Player's professional "quality" that Hamlet called for earlier. Hamlet's question, therefore, misses the point: "What would he do / Had he the motive and the cue for passion / That I have?" (2.2.570–72). What Hamlet cannot understand here is that the Player cannot do any more to express Hamlet's real passion than he does for Hecuba's fictive passion. The Player already has all the cues for passion that he needs, and Hamlet's ranting catalogue of exaggerated stage action only reinforces his own isolation from the passion that he himself needs. In fact, he sounds like the bad actor he warns against in his advice to the Players, tearing "a passion to tatters, to very rags, to split the ears of the groundlings" (3.2.10–11). Hamlet seems to have the cue and the desire for passion without the passion itself, so that his soliloquy becomes excessive, mere ranting without authenticity.

Although Hamlet calls for a passionate speech, he is clearly of divided minds about histrionic passion. In his exacting advice to the Players, he comes out strongly against passion. The actor must, above all, maintain control, "use all gently" (3.2.5), and not become completely absorbed in his role as the First Player does in speaking about Hecuba: "in the very torrent, tempest, and (as I may say) whirlwind of your passion, you must acquire and beget a temperance that may give it smoothness" (5–8). A smooth and gentle passion? That sounds like Bottom promising to roar "as gently as any sucking dove; I will roar you an 'twere any nightingale" (*A Midsummer Night's Dream* 1.2.82–84). In these paradoxes Hamlet's awareness of the doubleness of acting also has implications for his own acting of revenge. One must avoid the histrionic and that is why it offends Hamlet to his soul to "hear a robustious periwig-pated fellow tear a passion to tatters, to very rags, to split the ears of the groundlings" (3.2.9–11). Again, this sounds like Bottom offering to play "Ercles rarely, or a part to tear a cat in, to make all split" (*A Midsummer Night's Dream* 1.2.30–31). Hamlet's advice to the Players functions like advice to himself on how he should play to his own audience. Passion, the actor's motive force, must be excluded from performance, or at least there must be a temperance that governs the execution so that the actor does not wind up with "Tears in his eyes, distraction in his aspect" (2.2.565) and unable to continue. That is unprofessional.

In choosing Horatio as his confidant – and his confederate in the Play Scene – Hamlet wants a man "That is not passion's slave" (3.2.74). Hamlet's explanation of why his soul hath sealed Horatio for herself is embarrassingly full, and it bears an interesting analogy to the advice to the Players, which it immediately follows. The speech about Horatio defines those qualities of manliness that

Hamlet most admires but does not necessarily imitate. Horatio is the philosophical man superior to Fortune, "A man that Fortune's buffets and rewards / Hast ta'en with equal thanks" (69–70), an equable man, modest, temperate and gentle,

> Whose blood and judgment are so well commeddled
> That they are not a pipe for Fortune's finger
> To sound what stop she please.   (3.2.71–73)

Horatio has qualities surprisingly similar to those of the good actor; both are essentially rational and unheroic – always in control. This is not the path for the tragic protagonist, who must almost of necessity taint his mind by being passion's slave. There is a concentration, intensity, and obsessiveness in Hamlet that are needed for him to exist in a non-rational world. Without his passion Hamlet would be lost; with it he is nevertheless puzzled about how to connect strong feeling with action.

In the dumbshow of *The Mousetrap* play, we are told that the Queen *"makes passionate action"* (3.2.140 s.d.) when she finds the King dead. Because it is a stage direction, this example is omitted from Spevack's *Concordance*, although it sums up nicely the slippery character of the Player Queen: she is both passionate with grief and passionately amorous for the embraces of her lover/poisoner. The dumbshow is filled with passionate gesture, an exaggerated and stylized pantomime. The King and Queen enter *"very lovingly."* Then the Queen *"kneels; and makes show of protestation unto him."* Of course, it is only a "show," not real, like the Queen's later *"passionate action."* In the dialogue immediately following, "show" is repeated four times in punning senses. The frightened and cowed Ophelia asks, "Will 'a tell us what this show meant?" (148) and the swaggering Hamlet answers: "Ay, or any show that you will show him. Be not you ashamed to show, he'll not shame to tell you what it means" (149–51). This is "show" in the sense of "show and tell." Like Othello in the Brothel Scene (IV, ii), Hamlet is treating Ophelia like a whore.

The Player King already intuits his Queen's temperament when he objects to her protests against second marriage: "What to ourselves in passion we propose, / The passion ending, doth the purpose lose" (3.2.200–1). Again, we have a built-in pun on passion as strong emotion, either grief or amorousness. Our purposes therefore depend upon passion to be enacted, which resembles the King's nostalgic speech to Laertes about the nature of love: "There lives within the very flame of love / A kind of wick or snuff that will abate it" (4.7.114–15). Therefore we should follow our passion before it cools: "That we would do / We should do when we would" (118–19).

That may be the Ghost's voluntaristic point when it appears in the Closet Scene to chide its tardy son, "That, lapsed in time and passion, lets go by / Th' important acting of your dread command" (3.4.108–9). Why does Hamlet think himself lapsed in passion? Much depends on how we understand that theatrical word "passion." There is clearly a wrong and a right passion. For most of the play Hamlet is so preoccupied with the rhetoric of passion – the fiction and the dream of passion – that he has difficulty dealing with his true feelings apart from their inflamed expression. When Hamlet's revenge comes in the final scene of the play, it is different from anything he had previously imagined. And it is remarkably free of passionate rhetoric (as well as "passion" words).

We may notice two further examples of passion that are related to Ophelia, who is the most obvious slave of passion in the play; her madness expresses her unrequited and unrequitable passion. The complacent Polonius, who knows less than any other character about passion, warns his daughter against the effects of love as a mad passion, an "ecstasy,"

> Whose violent property fordoes itself
> And leads the will to desperate undertakings
> As oft as any passions under heaven
> That does afflict our natures.   (2.1.103–6)

Like father, like son. In an earlier scene Laertes had rather grossly warned his sister about opening her "chaste treasure" to Hamlet's "unmastered importunity" (1.3.31–32), as if the only protection against passion was: "Be wary then; best safety lies in fear" (1.3.43). In Ophelia's madness, Laertes cannot tolerate the fact that everything is so confused: "Thought and affliction, passion, hell itself, / She turns to favor and to prettiness" (4.5.186–87). Laertes would like everything to be clear and simple. Madness is not a possibility open to his humdrum soul, which is why he is so easily duped by the king.

All the "passion" examples in *Hamlet* seem to make the same point: passion is dangerous but without passion no great deeds can occur. There is a close link between passion and the heroic. Yet passion is eminently a word associated with the theater. The actor gives us a taste of his quality by enacting fictive passions, the loves and sorrows of others, as in Hecuba the "mobled queen," almost destroyed by the sight of Pyrrhus killing old Priam, her husband. Hamlet is teased and tempted by theatrical passion and its accompanying high-flown rhetoric, which at moments in the play he strives to outdo. He admires Horatio, the temperate and rational man, because he is so unlike Horatio. One of the most striking issues of the play is how life can imitate the theater, or at least how life can be made to seem real without losing its fiction and its dream of passion. The actor in the revenge plot is like the actor in the play: both must await the motive and the cue for passion.

Aside from the "passion" words in *Hamlet*, there are many other evocations of strong emotion that corroborate our ambivalent sense of the play. The strong feelings that are aroused tend also to be terrifying, and the characters don't always know what to do with their passionate excitement. This is one way to interpret Eliot's otherwise puzzling observation that the feelings in the play tend to be in excess of the facts, or that the characters, especially Hamlet, cannot process their "objective correlative."[3] There is an unusual degree of speech-making in the play, with its accompanying bombast and rant, as if to acknowledge that the rhetoric cannot adequately express the turbulence and intensity of feelings that are aroused. There is a gap between language and suffering.

Let us consider passion from the point of view of three characters besides Hamlet: the Ghost, Laertes, and Gertrude. The Ghost generates excitement whenever it appears, which may, of course, have been the Elizabethan convention about ghosts – that they must be portentous. It "harrows" the even-tempered Horatio "with fear and wonder" (1.1.44); he trembles and looks pale, and the watch is "distilled / Almost to jelly with the act of fear" (1.2.204–5). Hamlet's "wild and whirling words" (1.5.133) are a direct effect of the Ghost. Its appearance from beyond the grave bodes some strange eruption for the state. As Hamlet puts it, the Ghost makes us – "we fools of nature" – "So horridly to shake our disposition / With thoughts beyond the reaches of our souls" (1.4.54–56).

The emotions aroused are transcendental, or at least force the living audience to think of their mortality. Hamlet "waxes desperate with imagination" (1.4.87). In his effort to imagine the Ghost, he is also trying to imagine his own life and death. The Ghost releases powerful emotions, and its lurid hint of the "secrets" of its "prison house" will overwhelm young Hamlet:

> I could a tale unfold whose lightest word
> Would harrow up thy soul, freeze thy young blood,
> Make thy two eyes like stars start from their spheres . . . .
> (1.5.15–17)

This is the prologue to the Ghost's revelation of its murder. How could Hamlet not "taint" his mind (1.5.85) when he has heard so much and been confirmed in his most powerful and frightening fantasies both about his mother and his uncle? The passion is too great for Hamlet to control – "Hold, hold, my heart" (1.5.93) – so it must necessarily issue out in "wild and whirling words" (133) and an "antic disposition" (172). These are modes both for tempering and expressing passion.

Laertes' passion is manifested quite differently from Hamlet's. Like Tybalt in *Romeo and Juliet*, Laertes is almost a caricature of the Elizabethan revenger, and the figure of Pyrrhus in the Dido and Aeneas play parallels Laertes. In IV, vii the astute Claudius undoes Laertes' *coup d'état* and guides him through his revenger's catechism. Earlier, Laertes vowed revenge with powerful oaths and hyperboles. He scorns the Queen's command, "Calmly, good Laertes":

That drop of blood that's calm proclaims me bastard,
Cries cuckold to my father, brands the harlot
Even here between the chaste unsmirchèd brow
Of my true mother.   (4.5.117–20)

"Something too much of this" (3.2.76), as Hamlet says to Horatio.
Or, later, after the ranting Laertes has leaped into Ophelia's grave,
Hamlet asks: "What is he whose grief / Bears such an emphasis"
(5.1.256–57)? It is bad acting, "it out-herods Herod" (3.2.14–15).
Laertes equates real feeling with being womanish, but when his
tears have ended "The woman will be out" (4.7.189). In other
words, he will be a man again and no longer allowed to express
feeling.

Gertrude is a puzzling figure in the play, who only comes alive
in the Closet Scene (III,iv) and after. The upshot of this scene
occurs in the words of Claudius that follow immediately: "There's
matter in these sighs. These profound heaves / You must
translate" (4.1.1–2). For all his cruelty, Hamlet brings his mother
to some sort of emotional awareness. At first, he is horrified that
Gertrude seems without any sense perception at all: "Eyes without
feeling, feeling without sight, / Ears without hands or eyes,
smelling sans all" (3.4.79–80). The accusation of being insensate is
very strong, and it seems to be confirmed by Gertrude's failure to
see the Ghost, "yet all that is I see" (133). This is usually
interpreted as an example of spiritual blindness. Yet Hamlet has
cleft his mother's heart in twain, so that she may live "the purer
with the other half" (159). Clearly, Hamlet has been successful in
his determination to "wring" his mother's heart, "If it be made of
penetrable stuff" (37). From this moment on in the tragedy,
Gertrude, like Emilia in *Othello*, becomes an emotional factor that
must be reckoned with. She can no longer be taken for granted as
Claudius' dutiful but shallow wife.

There is much talk of heart in *Hamlet*, heart as the seat of the
emotions. Almost the very first words of the play are Francisco's
announcement that he is "sick at heart" (1.1.9). When Ophelia
goes mad, she "hems, and beats her heart" (4.5.5). In Hamlet's "To
be, or not to be" soliloquy, "to die, to sleep" will end "The

heartache, and the thousand natural shocks / That flesh is heir to"
(3.1.62–63). As he recounts to Horatio the story of the fateful
voyage to England: "Sir, in my heart there was a kind of fighting /
That would not let me sleep" (5.2.4–5). From Hamlet's heartache
and insomnia comes his spontaneous plan about how to save his
life. He is rescued by his own impetuosity – "Rashly / (And praised
be rashness for it)" (5.2.6–7). By following his passion "When our
deep plots do pall" (5.2.9), Hamlet manages to survive.

   Hamlet has always appealed to critics as Shakespeare's most
autobiographical play. If it is a mirror of Shakespeare, then how
much more so of the critic himself. Coleridge thought "I have a
smack of Hamlet myself, if I may say so,"[4] and Goethe wrote his
autobiographical sketch, *Wilhelm Meister* (1796), through the
medium of a production of *Hamlet*. Critics have a knack of finding
what they want to see in the play. Is Shakespeare Hamlet? If he is,
then he is a remarkably protean personality who can never be
fixed in a single attitude or interpretation. What is authorship if it
is not the projection of a series of images and fictions that grow out
of the author's own life? I do not mean to literalize the richness of
imagination to body forth meanings, yet these meanings have a
personal dimension. Passion and related affective words and
images in *Hamlet* are special to *Hamlet* and to Shakespeare. They
are not necessarily the expression of general truths.

   If Shakespeare were Hamlet – and how could he not be? – these
are some of the lessons of passion that must have passed through his
mind. "To be" carries with it the fearful obligations of the human
condition. It is curious how in this most famous of all soliloquies
the issues of what it means to stay alive are so intensely practical:
fardels and the law's delays, the pangs of despised love, the
insolence of office, and the spurns that patient merit must bear
from the unworthy. We seem to be feeling the author's outrage in
this passage. As a dramatist, Shakespeare was especially concerned
with his own art, as if there were a sharp distinction between the
actions that a man might play and what he felt that went beyond an
actor's "show." Hamlet is troubled by the actor's superiority in
fictive passion to his own clumsy and delayed enactment of his
own very real passions. In other words, it looks as if Shakespeare

realized that everything could be better done in a play than in real life, and we are meant to feel Hamlet's anguish about actualizing his dream of passion. The passion seems to be trapped by "thinking too precisely on th' event" (4.4.41).

2

How Pirandellian is Shakespeare?

Since there has been so much "throwing about of brains" (2.2.366–67) in *Hamlet*, it is not amiss that we should pose some speculative questions of our own about the relations of Pirandello and Shakespeare.[1] This is especially relevant to the question of passion. We are not primarily interested in how Shakespearean Pirandello is, although he obviously thought of Shakespeare as an important model, but rather in the other side of the equation: how Pirandellian is Shakespeare? The methodological question relates Shakespeare and Pirandello in assumptions about form and dramatic technique. It is an imaginative construct, yet there is an affinity of mind, passion, and theatrical method that offers a basis from which to begin. The Shakespearean and the Pirandellian are two analogous modes of a theatrical probing of reality and the ontological status of the play as a fiction, so that the plays of Shakespeare and Pirandello can be made to comment on each other. Most obviously, Pirandello's *Henry IV* has affinities with Shakespeare's *Hamlet*.[2] But the gender games of *The Taming of the Shrew* and its illusionistic frame are Pirandellian in their self-conscious exploitation of histrionic experience. In *A Midsummer Night's Dream* the imaginative displacements of the forest world are very much in the Pirandellian mode. In fact, all of Shakespeare's plays-within-plays are Pirandellian in their ironic assumptions.

But *Hamlet* and *Six Characters in Search of an Author* have a remarkable connection in their central experience. Both plays are speculative, rationalizing, passionate, and self-conscious. Their protagonists are great self-explainers and self-justifiers, but not always sympathetic. At times they go out of their way to alienate the audience, which reflects their largeness of conception – they needn't consistently be one thing or another. In both plays the main assumption is that one cannot separate life from the histrionic events of a play, since the two are equally plotted and unpredictable. But the play world reveals searing truths that would otherwise remain hidden, must remain hidden in the ordinary course of things. Truth is passionately conceived; it is not an abstraction. The characters press on to their doom despite their own relentless awareness of self-destruction. It is no coincidence that the actors in *Six Characters* are rehearsing Pirandello's *The Rules of the Game* when they are suddenly interrupted by the six characters. Leone Gala in *The Rules of the Game* is Pirandello's exemplar of the stoical man, who nevertheless suffers intensely from his forcibly willed separation from his wife. Like Hamlet, Leone values "the play of the intellect that clarifies the chaos of your passions, that outlines clearly and precisely all that moves within you so tumultuously."[3] But the intellect does not operate in some higher intellectual sphere of abstract ideas. The chaos of the passions is its natural arena, the mysterious world "that moves within you so tumultuously," in which the intellect functions as an animal tamer.

This prepares us for Leone's brilliant image of the passions as wild beasts, an image colored by the classical topos of Actaeon being torn apart by his own hounds:

> Do you think I have no feelings, no emotions? Of course I do. But I never let them get away from me. I seize them, I dominate them and I nail them up. Have you ever seen a trainer at work in a cage full of wild beasts? That's what I am, Silia: a lion tamer. But even as I play this part, I can stand aside and laugh at myself in my chosen role. And I confess that sometimes I have a terrible temptation to give in, to let myself be torn apart by one of these savage beasts. (p. 128)

It is typical of Pirandello to derogate the powers of reason and intellect. They are not powerful enough or masterful enough to rule the passions or to give a meaningful direction to one's life. Pirandello's *raisonneurs*, like Laudisi in *It Is So! (If You Think So)*, are always men of ironically limited vision because their rationality insulates them from the events they pretend to understand and, by not taking sides, they seem smug and complacent. They stand above and outside the tremendous events they comment on. *The Rules of the Game* lays the basis for understanding *Six Characters*, which develops from the earlier play. Now the six characters and not just Leone's wife demand their right to self-expression, which is tantamount to the right to be.

Hamlet, too, may be understood as an assault on the pretensions of human reason. One cannot shape one's destiny by an act of reason. One cannot through the mind control the flow of events. As Hamlet learns more about his situation, his world seems "an unweeded garden / That grows to seed. Things rank and gross in nature / Possess it merely" (1.2.135–37). The existence of evil mocks the power of reason – "O God, a beast that wants discourse of reason / Would have mourned longer" (150–51). In recalling Hamlet's outrage for his dead father, "But two months dead, nay, not so much, not two" (138), the Step-Daughter in *Six Characters* seems to echo Hamlet's soliloquy in her climactic incest scene:

> He is to ask me why I'm in mourning; and I'm to answer with tears in my eyes, that it is just two months since papa died. No sir, no! He's got to say to me; as he did say: "Well, let's take off this little dress at once." And I; with my two months' mourning in my heart, went there behind that screen, and with these fingers tingling with shame . . . .[4]

Like the events in *Hamlet*, everything in *Six Characters* seems melodramatic and overwrought. It is theatrical passion conscious of its own histrionics, yet also strangely moving. We believe not in the reasonableness of what is happening but in its intense irrationality and inevitability. In both plays the plot hammers at us. We are, as it were, involuntary spectators caught up like the Manager and his actors and the court of Elsinore in the irresistible pressure of events.

Pirandello's six characters are like the typical traveling company of Shakespeare's time, the sort of troupe that has taken to the road in *Hamlet* because of competition from the children's companies, the "little eyases" that "are most tyrannically clapped for't" (2.2.347–49). This situation is recapitulated in Tom Stoppard's *Rosencrantz and Guildenstern Are Dead*, but the details are left vague. Hamlet is like Pirandello's Manager in his concern for all the practical matters connected with the sudden appearance of the actors. Both plays move in the split reality of the play world and the real world. Pirandello's actors scorn the hokey reality of the characters, who make claims to truth and passion and authenticity that seem laughable to the professionals. In *Hamlet* the court of Elsinore mocks mere actors. Polonius, who plays the role of Master of the Revels, feels free to express his tutored disdain: "This is too long" (2.2.509). The court views the actors with skepticism and detachment. They are paid entertainers, so that when Hamlet transforms them into truth-speakers, the effect is explosive.

So in *Six Characters* the itinerant characters ensnare us in their overheated drama. We move gradually from disbelief to an awareness of their plight. In other words, we gradually abandon our defenses and agree to accept their fiction as true. But we never forget that the characters are enacting a soap opera with the most extravagant emotional assumptions. The mute Boy of fourteen, for example, accidentally displays the gun with which he will eventually kill himself, as the Step-Daughter perceives him in her hysterical frenzy:

> What have you got there? What are you hiding? [*Pulls his hand out of his pocket, looks into it and catches the glint of a revolver.*] Ah! where did you get this? [*The* BOY, *very pale in the face, looks at her, but does not answer.*] Idiot! If I'd been in your place, instead of killing myself, I'd have shot one of those two, or both of them: father and son.   (p. 238)

We are moving to the inevitable climax in which the Boy shoots himself and the little girl of four drowns herself in the fountain. Is it pretence or is it reality? The Father, "*with a terrible cry,*" exclaims: "Pretence? Reality, sir, reality!" (p. 276). But it is the characters' reality and not that of the real world, and we are to understand, I think, that the six characters will continue to enact their family drama without any regard to the limitations of time, space, and mortality.

We already know from the Mother that the Step-Daughter has run away, but the six characters are an integral and timeless group. Their story is taking place in an eternal present which has no relation to past or future: they are enacting their critical moment, their apotheosis, their big scene. As the Mother puts it:

> It's taking place now. It happens all the time. My torment isn't a pretended one. I live and feel every minute of my torture. Those two children there – have you heard them speak? They can't speak any more. They cling to me to keep up my torment actual and vivid for me. But for themselves, they do not exist, they aren't any more. And she [*Indicating the* STEP-DAUGHTER.] has run away, she has left me, and is lost. If I now see her here before me, it is only to renew for me the tortures I have suffered for her too.   (p. 260)

But this is, of course, the most teasing point. In what sense do the characters feel? In what acutely painful sense is their drama taking place now? How is the enactment related to the reality? The Father reiterates the histrionic paradox:

> The eternal moment! She [*Indicating the* STEP-DAUGHTER.] is here to catch me, fix me, and hold me eternally in the stocks for that one fleeting and shameful moment of my life. She can't give it up! And you sir [the Manager], cannot either fairly spare me it.   (p. 260)

The Father insists on his passion, on that moment of confrontation with the Step-Daughter in the brothel that so excruciatingly defines his shame. He will not be cheated out of the most critical climax of his role. Without these special histrionic moments the characters lose their being and their *raison d'être*. Their total experience is limited to the life of the play they are enacting.

We think of the Player's Speech in *Hamlet*, in which the passions are so ceremoniously buried in archaic rhetoric. Yet through the thickets of formal declamation, we manage to feel for Hecuba's tragic fate. The extravagant antitheses frame an emotion that is ready to burst: she may threaten the flames of burning Troy with her own "bisson rheum" or blinding tears, "a clout upon that head / Where late the diadem stood" (2.2.517–18), but she is nevertheless an emblem of overpowering grief. The melodramatic style of Pirandello and the archaistic rhetoric of Shakespeare both tend to assuage our torment. These displacing styles keep grief at a distance. We can comfortably feel both apart and superior, as the Manager and his cast look with disdain on these dubious, old-fashioned characters, making so much noise about their truth and their authenticity.

But the declaiming Player in *Hamlet* gets caught up in Hecuba's passion and has to cut short his speech: "Look, whe'r he has not turned his color, and has tears in's eyes" (2.2.530–31). Hamlet then catches this contagious passion of the Player, but he cannot understand what is happening to him:

> Is it not monstrous that this player here,
> But in a fiction, in a dream of passion,
> Could force his soul so to his own conceit . . . .
> (2.2.561–63)

The Player's fiction and dream of passion are strikingly close to those of the six characters in Pirandello, whose grief is also overwrought. But in what sense is it "all for nothing" (567)? It still remains for Hamlet to discover that it is not all for nothing, "For Hecuba!" (568), as he exclaims so disdainfully, a mere Hecuba. By the end of this soliloquy, Hamlet is already putting greater faith in the power of a histrionic illusion to catch the conscience of the King.

If we see Stoppard's *Rosencrantz and Guildenstern Are Dead* as part of an extended *Hamlet – Hamlet* as cultural artifact – then we can perceive some further implications of the secret life of the Players. Guildenstern is baffled by the Player's nonchalance, so that it is never possible to discern at what point the actor is once more a person. The Player's answers to Guildenstern are disingenuously sincere, but Guildenstern understands them as an expression of metaphysical terrors:

> GUIL. Well . . . aren't you going to change into your costume?
> PLAYER. I never change out of it, sir.
> GUIL. Always in character.
> PLAYER. That's it.
>   (*Pause.*)
> GUIL. Aren't you going to – come *on*?
> PLAYER. I *am* on.
> GUIL. But if you *are* on, you can't *come* on. *Can* you?
> PLAYER. I *start* on.
> GUIL. But it hasn't *started.*[5]

The answer, of course, is that the Player is not a person, just as the characters in Pirandello insist that they are characters and not persons. They too start on and fully costumed – they are always in their play and do not have to come on as other characters do.

But this is an unsatisfactory answer because Shakespeare, Pirandello, and Stoppard deliberately cloak their actors and players and characters in ambiguities that cannot be resolved. The play world and the real world are hopelessly confounded. Does the boy really shoot himself and the little girl drown herself in *Six Characters*, or can the Player die in *Rosencrantz and Guildenstern Are Dead*? In the unromantic world of Stoppard death means only that you exit without re-entering, but Guildenstern still feels that there is a passionate distinction between himself and the Player:

> I'm talking about death – and you've never experienced *that*. And you cannot *act* it. You die a thousand casual deaths – with none of that intensity which squeezes out life . . . and no blood runs cold anywhere. Because even as you die you know that you will come back in a different hat. But no one gets up after *death* – there is no applause – there is only silence and some second-hand clothes, and that's – *death* – . . . .　　　　　　(p. 213)

Yet even Guildenstern, who faces his imminent disappearance in the next few moments, cannot successfully distinguish between what is death on stage and off. The silence and second-hand clothes he mentions are suspiciously histrionic.

Shakespeare, Pirandello, and Stoppard share a distrust for

naturalistic drama. They are constantly breaking the illusion and playing with the audience's expectations. It is only a play, and, as Hamlet exclaims so ironically, "No, no, they do but jest, poison in jest; no offense i' th' world" (3.2.240–41). *The Murder of Gonzago* "is the image of a murder done in Vienna" (244), it is *The Mousetrap* play, "but what of that?" The play is an illusion to those who have the good conscience to think so. "Your majesty, and we that have free souls, it touches us not. Let the galled jade winch; our withers are unwrung" (247–49). In *Henry IV, Part One*, Cut is a galled jade who is "wrung in the withers out of all cess" (2.1.6–7); in other words, the horse's shoulders are rubbed raw in an extreme degree. "Let the galled jade winch (or wince)" is a proverbial expression for uncovering guilt, but in *The Mousetrap* we are all "guilty creatures sitting at a play" (2.2.601), so that even the most patently histrionic and melodramatic illusion makes us cry out in pain.

In *Six Characters* it is when the Manager and his actors abandon their protective superciliousness that we are ready for the catastrophe. They can no longer deny their complicity in the ridiculous events that are unfolding before them. And in Stoppard, Rosencrantz and Guildenstern's terror does not permit the players to expatiate freely in their roles. The courtiers' own fear of death sets limits to the histrionic illusion:

> Actors! The mechanics of cheap melodrama! That isn't *death*! . . . No, no, no . . . you've got it all wrong . . . you can't act death. The *fact* of it is nothing to do with seeing it happen – it's not gasps and blood and falling about – that isn't what makes it death. It's just a man failing to reappear, that's all . . . an exit, unobtrusive and unannounced, a disappearance gathering weight as it goes on, until, finally, it is heavy with death.
>
> (pp. 83–84)

But even in Guildenstern's pitiful reasoning, he is merely distinguishing between acting death well and acting it badly.

Stoppard is overtly Pirandellian in his conflation of illusion and reality and his refusal to distinguish between the play world and the real world. But where shall we place Shakespeare? In *Hamlet* we are in no doubt about the boundaries of the play world and the

real world, yet the Player's Speech about Aeneas and Dido as well
as *The Mousetrap* play make a strenuous demonstration of Hamlet's
reality right in the midst of Shakespeare's play. Now that it is no
longer fashionable to think of Shakespeare as primarily a learned
man, we can begin to see some *rapprochement* between Shakespeare
and Pirandello, who also had enormous intellectual curiosity
without being learned in an academic sense. Pirandello seems to
glorify thinking men, but when we look closer the thinking men
always turn out to believe not in abstractions or ideology or even
the powers of reason, but rather in the validity of complex
feelings. Shakespeare, too, has no intellectuals as such, but only
characters like Hamlet and Macbeth who think intensely about
moral and experiential truths.

Shakespeare would certainly have agreed with Pirandello when
he speaks of the profound source of humor in *"il sentimento del
contrario"* ("the feeling of the opposite").[6] This "reconciliation of
opposites," in Coleridge's commendatory term for Shakespeare's
genius, refuses the dualism that separates intellect and passion. It is
like Eliot's "unified sensibility," or, to put it in Pirandello's own
terms: "One of the novelties that I have given to the modern
drama consists in converting the intellect into passion."[7] It is along
these lines that we must see the relation of Pirandello and
Shakespeare. Both men were not afraid of a certain wildness and
frenzy in their imaginings. Perhaps they both liked to take things
too far and to cultivate excess as a virtue in its own right, but in
both Shakespeare and Pirandello there is an extraordinary insight
into how the world of the play impinges on truth and reality. In
both writers the play metaphor is central. There is also a curious
and unanticipated link between Shakespeare's Stratford-on-Avon
in England and Pirandello's Girgenti in Sicily. English and Sicilian
folklore overlap in their concern for the life of the passions and the
pleasures of illusion, and both demonstrate an almost uncontrol-
lable urge for personal honor and integrity.

3

Ophelia and other madwomen in Elizabethan plays

Madness is the most obvious expression of passion in Shakespeare, a disordered passion that breaks the narrow bounds of reason and civilized constraints. Mad characters on the Elizabethan stage all have their own special language, costume, and gesture, which depend on a set of theatrical conventions about how to represent madness effectively. These assumptions and expectations are as stylized as those, for example, that govern the staging of ghosts and drunkards as well as a variety of ethnic types (some of whom are seen with full-blown accents and mannerisms in Shakespeare's *Henry V*). Madwomen are much more strongly defined on stage than madmen. Madness allows women an emotional intensity and scope not usually expected in conventional feminine roles. Their madness is interpreted as a specifically feminine condition, a release from gender constraints, whereas the madness of men is not considered something specifically male.

The madwomen of Shakespeare and his fellow dramatists need to be understood in their contemporary context and especially within the cultural assumptions about women built into the language. Any strong expression of emotion is thought to be womanish. As Laertes says of his tears for the dead Ophelia, "When these are gone, / The woman will be out" (4.7.188–89). In other words, once he has finished weeping, he will have fully expressed the feminine side of his nature. He is not proud of his weakness; it is shameful for a man to act like a woman. In Elizabethan physiology, hysteria was specifically associated with women and was thought to be caused by a malfunction of the womb (from the Greek *hystera*, which means uterus or womb).

Hysteria was called familiarly "the mother," as in Lear's passionate attempt to master his imminent madness: "O, how this mother swells up toward my heart! / Hysterica passio, down, thou climbing sorrow" (*King Lear* 2.4.55–56). Like the rising gorge to indicate vomiting, the rising "mother" is an unpropitious physiological sign.

The madness of women in Elizabethan drama is usually brought on by "the pangs of despised love" (*Hamlet* 3.1.72). Love melancholy fills a whole section of Burton's *Anatomy of Melancholy* (1621) – its causes, its symptoms, and its cure – and Burton is particularly sympathetic to those whose problems arise from sexual inhibition and repression, as in the account of nuns' melancholy. The exact degrees of love melancholy are difficult to determine, but once the "humours" (the four essential bodily fluids) are burnt (or "adust"), pathology sets in. This pathology may be either neurotic or psychotic – Renaissance authors did not insist on a firm distinction between the two – and "madness" tends to include a wide variety of symptoms.[1] Thus "distracted" and "mad" are used synonymously, although "distracted" is a milder term. "Lunatic," a strong word, is not so common; according to the Spevack *Concordance*, Shakespeare uses it (and related forms) 19 times. "Frenzy" is another strong term (14 examples) as well as its related adjective "frantic" (17 examples). "Fit" as a noun (22 occurrences, not all related to madness) could be used rather vaguely in combinations, such as the "frantic fit" or "lunatic fit." The strongest word for madness in Shakespare is "ecstasy" (16 examples) to indicate a sudden fit in which the soul is imagined to be separated from the body (as, for example, in a mystical state, either erotic or religious). The mildest madness words are those related to "dotage" (15 examples) and "dote" (45 examples), many of which do not specifically indicate madness at all, but rather an advanced state of foolishness associated with old age. In popular parlance, "lunacy," "ecstasy," "frenzy," and "dotage" could all be used as generalized (and sometimes comic) equivalents of "madness."

The mad Ophelia is the prototype of a great many madwomen to follow, who scrupulously imitate her style. She is close to nature, as indicated in her flower imagery and her concern for natural processes, but it is a nature full of folklore perils, especially the danger of self-annihilation.[2] Her speech is childlike in both matter and manner, from which she draws a fund of pathos from the audience – "Her mood will needs be pitied" (4.5.3). She sings snatches of old ballads, as Hamlet does after his triumph with the *Mousetrap* play. But Ophelia's ballads are preoccupied with her own explosive sexuality:

> Then up he rose and donned his clothes
>> And dupped [opened] the chamber door,
> Let in the maid, that out a maid
>> Never departed more.   (4.5.52–55)

> Young men will do't if they come to't,
>> By Cock, they are to blame. (4.5.60–61)

Where could the proper and well brought up Ophelia have learned these bawdy songs?

The mad Ophelia finds it easier to sing than to speak, and her discourse and syntax are fragmentary and broken. Her speeches are organized by lyrical free association, with many veiled innuendos and pointed allusions to the state of affairs in Denmark. "My brother shall know of it" (4.5.70–71), she says menacingly to the King, who is worried by what she may let slip: "Follow her close; give her good watch, I pray you" (74). There is an interesting analogy between the mad Ophelia and the supposedly mad Hamlet, both of whom make the exceedingly careful and rational Claudius very nervous: "Madness in great ones must not unwatched go" (3.1.191). The King is preoccupied with voyeurism and exhibitionism, which express themselves in the form of surveillance. He wants to keep an eye on what everyone is doing, and he wants everyone to take notice of his public image, as "white as snow" (3.3.47).

The loss of rationality in Ophelia is expressed by a shift from verse to prose, as if blank verse were too orderly a medium in which to couch her wild fancies. Shakespeare might have learned to represent madness as a sudden shift from verse to prose from

Marlowe's Zabina in *Tamburlaine, Part I*, perhaps the first mad-woman in Elizabethan drama (although the mad Isabella in *The Spanish Tragedy* may also date from the same year, 1587). Zabina is crazed by extreme grief in seeing her husband, Bajazeth, knock his brains out against his cage. She does not go mad instantaneously but takes five exclamatory lines of Marlovian blank verse to lose her wits. Zabina's highly wrought mad style is a rhetorical display piece:

> Give him his liquor? Not I, bring milk and fire, and my blood I bring him againe, teare me in peeces, give me the sworde with a ball of wildefire upon it. Downe with him, downe with him. Goe to, my child, away, away, away. Ah, save that Infant, save him, save him. I, even I speak to her. The Sun was downe. Streamers white, Red, Blacke. Here, here, here. Fling the meat in his face. *Tamburlaine, Tamburlaine.* Let the souldiers be buried. Hel, death, *Tamburlaine*, Hell. Make ready my Coch, my chaire, my jewels, I come, I come, I come. (5.1.310–18)[3]

In an emotional frenzy, "*She runs against the Cage and braines her selfe.*" In anticipation of Tennessee Williams's more highly colored "memory" technique (as in *The Glass Menagerie*), Marlowe uses madness to dislodge fragments of remembered images. Ophelia echoes Zabina's "Make ready my Coch" in the line "Come, my coach!" (4.5.72), but Zabina is wilder than Ophelia, her imaginative leaps and repetitions more emphatic. Her single mad soliloquy is an operatic aria whereas Ophelia shows much greater variety and engages in poignant dialogue. Both characters are suddenly freed by madness from their completely conventional female roles.

The strong sexual and maternal imagery of Zabina and Ophelia is politely echoed by the Jailer's Daughter in *The Two Noble Kinsmen*, a late play generally attributed to Shakespeare and Fletcher. The madness of the Jailer's Daughter is specifically modeled on Ophelia's, except that it is almost purely ornamental – an occasion for pretty discourse rather than a soul-ravaging disorder. As she flees her father and misses her rendezvous with her beloved Palamon, whom she has freed from prison, she falls into charming hallucinations, in which she animates nature in the style of a child's fable:

> Would I could find a fine frog; he would tell me
> News from all parts o' th' world; then would I make
> A carack of a cockleshell, and sail
> By east and north-east to the King of Pigmies,
> For he tells fortunes rarely.   (3.4.12–16)

As the Doctor puts it so energetically, "How her brain coins!" (4.3.40), and "What stuff she utters!" (5.2.67). The Jailer's Daughter is the most extensively developed madwoman in all of Elizabethan drama, and her cure is effected with a fullness and specificity that leave little to the imagination. In short, since " 'tis not an engraffed madness, but a most thick and profound melancholy" (4.3.49–51), she can be restored to her wits only by the generous sexual activity denied her by Palamon but supplied without stinting by the anonymous gentleman called simply Wooer. Unlike Ophelia, the Jailer's Daughter can be saved by the psychological workings of tragicomedy.

The Doctor in this play has typically folkloristic views about the powers of sex: "Please her appetite / And do it home: it cures her *ipso facto* / The melancholy humor that infects her" (5.2.35–37). This is the traditional folk motif of "sickness (madness) cured by coition."[4] *The Two Noble Kinsmen* uses the madwoman motif in an almost completely conventional way, without exploring any psychological nuances. The Doctor, and more specifically the alienist-doctor (like our modern psychoanalyst), was a familiar figure on the Elizabethan stage. He is nowhere more vigorously represented than in Webster's *The Duchess of Malfi*, where, if all else fails, he threatens to "buffet" Ferdinand's "madness out of him" (5.2.26)[5] – an early anticipation of shock treatment. Ophelia has no doctor who can "minister to a mind diseased" (*Macbeth* 5.3.40), but must suffer a watery death brought on by her own inability to care for herself.

Ophelia is, in some ways, Shakespeare's most pitiable heroine. She is not witty and charming like the heroines of comedy, especially Rosalind, nor does she have Juliet's resourcefulness and

independence. There is no sense in which Ophelia may be said to
grow up in the course of the play. In her first appearance in Act I,
Scene iii, a domestic, family scene with her brother and her father,
she is bullied by Laertes and Polonius alike. She is mostly a listener
in this scene, which concerns itself directly with her love affair
with Hamlet. In answer to her father's irritating, catechistical
questions, she can only say: "I do not know, my lord, what I should
think" (1.3.104), which leads immediately to her father's total
control: "Marry, I will teach you. Think yourself a baby" (105).
We all remember the "few precepts" (28) that Polonius so self-
importantly gives his son, but we tend to forget the tedious weight
of precepts by which both father and son overwhelm Ophelia. She
ends the scene with a total submission uncharacteristic of a
Shakespearean heroine: "I shall obey, my lord" (136). Later, to test
Hamlet, Polonius will "loose" (2.2.162) his daughter to him.
When the testing is over and Ophelia has been cruelly abused in
the Nunnery Scene, Polonius dismisses her without any opportunity
for her to speak: "How now, Ophelia? / You need not tell us what
Lord Hamlet said; / We heard it all" (3.1.181–83). She is a mere
pawn in her father's plans.

There is no way to account directly for Ophelia's madness. She
is the dutiful daughter who will not contradict her father's and her
brother's wishes. If Ophelia's mother were present, these scenes of
psychological coercion would have a different quality, as Juliet's
mother and the nurse mitigate male tyranny. Ophelia goes mad
ostensibly from grief for her father's sudden murder, but parental
themes are interwoven with sexual themes and it is difficult to
separate frustrated love in all of its manifestations. Juliet, too, is
faced with the dilemma that her relative Tybalt has been killed by
her lover Romeo. Critics have been intrigued with the idea of
postulating some secret sexual guilt for Ophelia, especially a
hidden liaison with Claudius, with or without offspring.[6] We
don't need any specifically lurid or traumatic event to understand
Ophelia's overpowering feeling of guilt, her intense sense of
helplessness, and the inability to cope with affairs of state.

Lady Macbeth is an analogue to Ophelia in the sense that both
characters suffer acutely from general anxiety and guilt. Lady

Macbeth's sleepwalking scene (V,i) is also a mad scene, in which she speaks in the free-associational, non-rational, broken discourse we have come to expect from Elizabethan madwomen. Her fancy plays compulsively on the forbidden acts she cannot express directly. This is the highly charged language of dreams that figures in Freud's *The Interpretation of Dreams* (1900). Her hands cannot be washed clean of the blood that has stained them – the characteristic gesture of the scene is the attempt to wash away imaginary spots that will not disappear – and she speaks throughout to her husband, who she thinks is with her. Her hallucinations echo a bloody reality that is only too emphatically true.

Under these circumstances, Macbeth understands with chilling clarity that his questions to the doctor are purely rhetorical:

> Canst thou not minister to a mind diseased,
> Pluck from the memory a rooted sorrow,
> Raze out the written troubles of the brain,
> And with some sweet oblivious antidote
> Cleanse the stuffed bosom of that perilous stuff
> Which weighs upon the heart?
> (*Macbeth* 5.3.40–45)

Those who pity the mad Ophelia – Laertes, Gertrude, Horatio, perhaps even Claudius – might have asked the same questions, which indicate the need for psychiatric intervention. Madness is related to the sorrow rooted in the memory, it is a mental and spiritual condition written on the brain (as if it were a *tabula rasa*), perilous stuff that congests the bosom and weighs upon the heart. All of the terms are fully comprehensible in modern psychological parlance, and it is remarkable that Shakespeare should have had such an exact sense of the right terminology. Both Lady Macbeth and Ophelia are victims of inner perturbation, which finds a natural outlet in madness. Brutus' Portia likewise fell distract at the enormity of the secrets she had to conceal and "swallowed fire" (*Julius Caesar* 4.3.153); according to Plutarch, she killed herself by putting hot coals into her mouth.

"Some sweet oblivious antidote" in Macbeth's speech – some pleasant remedy that cures madness by physical means – recalls the

Doctor's remarkable cure in *The Two Noble Kinsmen*, but there seems to be an absolute separation between the madwomen in comedy and in tragedy. In comedy, all is usually recoverable, even one's wits, and an episode of madness may prove to be a valuable educational experience. Thus Pandora, in Lyly's *The Woman in the Moone*, goes through a "lunaticke" phase in Act V under the influence of Luna (or Cynthia). She becomes "new fangled, fyckle, slothfull, foolish, mad" (5.1.5), "idle, mutable, / Forgetfull, foolish, fickle, franticke, madde" (307–8).[7] These are the "humours" that content her best, but, once they are displayed and she becomes "sober" again, she chooses to remain with Cynthia as the woman in the moon.

During her mad fit, Pandora can fully indulge feminine caprices that are not only whimsical but also highly lyrical:

> Where is the larks? come, weel go catch some streight!
> No, let vs go a fishing with a net!
> With a net? no, an angle is enough:
> An angle, a net, no none of both,
> Ile wade into the water, water is fayre,
> And stroke the fishes vnder neath the gilles. (5.1.25–30)

Her sensuality, volatile and siren-like, anticipates the bored Cleopatra of Act II, Scene v of Shakespeare's play. Ophelia's mad scene (IV,v) is clearly indebted to Lyly in the sense that it too is a display piece of lyric inventiveness, but Shakespeare's scene is more closely integrated into the dramatic structure of *Hamlet*.

In the stage iconography of madness, no external sign is more familiar and more often repeated than that of a woman with her hair down,[8] virtually an emblem of madwomen on the Elizabethan stage. Ophelia enters *"distracted"* in the Folio stage direction (at 4.5.20), but the First Quarto of 1603 has a much more graphic indication: Enter Ophelia *"playing on a Lute, and her haire downe singing."*[9] Music, especially the singing of old, wistful, sentimental, and sometimes bawdy ballads, is both a frequent accompaniment of madness (an indication that rational discourse has broken down) and also one of the specific cures for disordered wits (as in *King Lear* 4.7.25). We know that Ophelia here is singing bits and pieces of popular love ballads, as in her death scene by drowning "she chanted snatches of old lauds" (4.7.177), or hymns. Does she accompany herself on the lute, a notoriously difficult instrument to play, or is she excused by reason of madness from playing at all? Or does she, perhaps, play in a mad and distracted style, which might be very effective theatrically? We are grateful to the "bad" quartos for giving us stage directions that seem to record contemporary stage business, directions that are missing in the more formal texts. Ophelia is suffering from the classic symptoms of love melancholy as described in Burton's *Anatomy of Melancholy*, and her grief for her father is compounded by her broken love affair with Hamlet.

We know at once that Ophelia is distracted because her hair is down. Instead of being put up on the "tire," or ornamental wire frame on which proper ladies arranged their elaborate coiffures, her hair has been let down; it is loose, disordered, disheveled. Shakespeare must have known a good deal about tires, since we know that he boarded with a French Huguenot tire-maker, Christopher Mountjoy, on the northeast corner of Muggle and Silver Streets in London around the year 1604,[10] close to the time he wrote *Hamlet*. For a lady to have her hair down is an offence against social decorum similar to Hamlet's sudden appearance in Ophelia's closet while she is sewing:

> his doublet all unbraced,
> No hat upon his head, his stockings fouled,
> Ungartered, and down-gyvèd to his ankle ....
> (2.1.78–80)

Polonius imagines that Ophelia's recent rejection of Hamlet has rendered him mad, with the appropriate derangement of his attire.

In *Troilus and Cressida*, Cassandra, "our mad sister" as Troilus calls her, enters "*raving, with her hair about her ears*" (2.2.96 s.d.), which gives an especially dire quality to her prophecies of Trojan doom, since mad persons were supposed to be psychically in tune with the future. In Marston's extravagant play, *Antonio's Revenge*, Maria appears with "*her hair loose*" (3.2. s.d.),[11] and the foolish Balurdo would "kiss the curled locks of your loose hair" (3.2.19).

Like the rank, unweeded garden of Hamlet's first soliloquy (1.2.135) and the disordered garden-commonwealth of *Richard II*, loose hair is an offense against decorum and therefore against the whole hierarchy of orderly correspondences. It is so improper and so overtly sensual that it may conventionally be understood to indicate a loss of reason, either temporary or permanent.

A thin line separates heightened emotion on the Elizabethan stage from distraction. Constance, the grieving mother of young Arthur in *King John*, is clearly not mad in our sense of the term, yet her loose hair expresses an excessive grief that is the subject of a little set piece of rhetorical elaboration. The conceit on binding and loosing is so artificial that the whole passage sounds like parody. King Philip of France begins:

> Bind up those tresses! O, what love I note
> In that fair multitude of those her hairs!
> Where but by chance a silver drop [=tear] hath fall'n,
> Even to that drop ten thousand wiry friends
> Do glue themselves in sociable grief . . . .
> (*King John* 3.3.61–65)

With insufferable fullness, Constance completes the figure of binding up her hairs:

> Yes, that I will; and wherefore will I do it?
> I tore them from their bonds and cried aloud,
> "O that these hands could so redeem my son,
> As they have given these hairs their liberty!"
> But now I envy at their liberty,
> And will again commit them to their bonds,
> Because my poor child is a prisoner.
> (*King John* 3.3.69–75)

This is like the "sorrow and grief of heart" that makes Richard II "speak fondly like a frantic man" (*Richard II* 3.3.183–84). The hair image in *King John* could be used with such complete detail because the audience would readily grasp its emblematic nature.

On the Elizabethan stage boy actors understood the conventions of playing madwomen and could respond spontaneously to the stage business and gesture required for the part. Otherwise, how are we to interpret a stage direction so cryptic and so compressed as the one for Isabella in *The Spanish Tragedy*: "*She runs lunatic*" (4.1.5 s.d.)?[12] Without any warning, the grief-stricken mother of the murdered Horatio suddenly goes into her mad role. "*She runs lunatic*" is a practical and specific stage direction, fully comprehensible to the actor, and not just a general invitation to ad-lib. There is a similar example in Webster's *The White Devil*: "CORNELIA *doth this in several forms of distraction*" (5.4.83 s.d.).[13] Webster presumably knows that there are various ways, besides the Ophelia-like language of her part, for the grief-crazed Cornelia to express her distraction. Mad folk have sudden starts; whims, cranks, and windmills in their brains; paranoid fears and hallucinations; spirits pursuing them; instructions from unseen powers. They are giddy, fantastic, apish, self-willed, and wild. All of these qualities demand a certain style of acting: spasmodic, lyrical, and intuitive. Even madness has its appropriate decorum – its "answering style."

We can best pursue this argument about the conventional inventory of the mad style with the many women who feign madness for some special purpose. In Fletcher's *The Pilgrim*, Alinda is able to conceal herself from her own father by playing mad:

ALPHONSO. Dost thou dwell in Segovia, Fool?
ALINDA. No, no, I dwell in Heaven;
    And I have a fine little house, made of marmalade,
    And I am a lone woman, and I spin for Saint Peter;
    I have a hundred little children, and they sing psalms with me.
                         (4.1)[14]

Alinda is so successful in her disguise because she has mastered the pretty, fanciful, childlike style and manner associated with mad girls. Free association produces an extravagance of metaphor, and the mad speeches often make little separable arias. The mad style offers a way of combining the lunatic, the lover, and the poet of Duke Theseus' speech in *A Midsummer Night's Dream*: their "seething brains" and "shaping fantasies" "apprehend / More than cool reason ever comprehends" (5.1.4–6).

The most frenzied (and most poetic) example of feigned madness is in Middleton and Rowley's *The Changeling*. Isabella, the young wife of the old and foolish Alibius, offers herself to Antonio, who is also feigning madness in the private sanatorium of Alibius. In typical fashion, Isabella's madness is strongly sexual, both in its overt intent and in its covert meanings. She pretends that her lover is Icarus at the very moment that he is falling into the sea, and her hallucination is made vividly dramatic – a fully realized enactment of "fear of flying":

> Art thou not drowned?
> About thy head I saw a heap of clouds
> Wrapped like a Turkish turbant: on thy back
> A crook'd chameleon-colored rainbow hung
> Like a tiara down unto thy hams.
> Let me suck out those billows in thy belly;
> Hark, how they roar and rumble in the streets!
> Bless thee from the pirates!   (4.3.131–38)[15]

This seems to echo Edgar's speech to Gloucester on Dover Cliffs in *King Lear* (4.6). On the prosaic Antonio, however, Isabella's lyrical assault is completely wasted. He protests, "Pox upon you, let me alone!" (138), and, more violently, "I'll kick thee, if again thou touch me, / Thou wild unshapen antic; I am no fool, / You bedlam!" (145–47). Antonio loses the very ready and willing Isabella, eager to "tread the lower labyrinth" (129), from failure of imagination. We discover imaginative gifts in the "mad" Isabella that make Antonio wholly unworthy of her.

The mad Ophelia is able to draw on an entirely different range of experience from what was available to her as only daughter of the chief counselor of Denmark. In her earlier career, Ophelia is polite and passive, the dutiful daughter who is "loosed" to Hamlet as a mere pawn in her father's plans. Her madness opens up her role, and she is suddenly lyric, poignant, pathetic, tragic. Madness enables her to assert herself and to express depths of feeling previously unknown. By tragic convention she need no longer be the silent woman, an inexpressive listener like Horatio, who is "one, in suff'ring all, that suffers nothing," a person "that

Fortune's buffets and rewards / Hast ta'en with equal thanks" (3.2.68–70). In her madness Ophelia comes alive as a character and becomes important in the play. Everyone is suddenly starting to worry about her and her secret power.

Madwomen offered Shakespeare and his fellow dramatists an opportunity to write speeches of exuberant fancy and lyric grace. They also provided a sanction for witty sexual innuendo and outright bawdy, since love melancholy could be pathetic, pretty, and sensual all at the same time. If the madwoman was a conventional role on the Elizabethan stage, it was unconventional – and perhaps even disturbing – in its exploration of feminine consciousness. Through madness, the women on stage can suddenly make a forceful assertion of their being. The lyric form and broken syntax and unbridled imagination all show ways of breaking through unbearable social restraints. Just as Shakespeare drew on earlier examples of madwomen in Kyd, Marlowe, Lyly, and others, so the role of Ophelia served as a model for all later madwomen on the Elizabethan stage. Ophelia distributing wildflowers, Ophelia singing bawdy ballads, Ophelia grieving for her dead father and her lost love – all this was unforgettable in its tragic poignancy.

We may conclude from our examples that madness on the Elizabethan stage releases the emotional and imaginative powers that the saner women in the play are required to suppress. To put it in a different way, it would seem that only imaginative women have the capacity for either true or feigned madness. There is an art in madness by which a character may bring her imaginative energies to fruition. In some direct way, madness fictionalizes dramatic characters and allows them to speak in a free, meandering discourse full of veiled significances. In her madness, we must pay attention to Ophelia, the dutiful daughter. The literary and theatrical problems of how madwomen express themselves in Shakespeare and his fellow dramatists overlap with the more general problems so polemically formulated in Phyllis Chesler's study, *Women and Madness* (1972). In the larger context, we need to work through this question of how women are used symbolically and what sort of release madness offers.

4

Hamlet's O-groans and textual criticism

Madness is a passionate occasion in drama and demands a passionate style. So too is death, yet there is a certain blandness in critics who would like death in Shakespeare to be a rhetorical occasion without unnecessary emotive expression. I would like to look specifically at the fate of O-groans in Shakespeare as an indication of death and examine why they have so generally disappeared from our modern texts. So much scorn has been heaped on Hamlet's last words in the Folio text – "O, o, o, o" (Norton 3847)[1] – that I hesitate to reopen this painful subject. Perhaps we should just let Hamlet die metaphorically with "The rest is silence" and let it go at that. Mardian reports that Cleopatra died in the very act of speaking the name of Antony:

> Then in the midst a tearing groan did break
> The name of Antony; it was divided
> Between her heart and lips: she rend'red life,
> Thy name so buried in her.
>
> (*Antony and Cleopatra* 4.14.31–34)

That is a grand death, so grand in fact that it never takes place and serves instead as a rhetorical model for how to die well. But "O, o, o, o"? Dover Wilson quotes Dowden's disapproval of these "unhappy" "O's" and goes on to inveigh against "little ejaculatory words or phrases which a player in the excitement of performance would be likely to add to his lines." "O, o, o, o" is "preposterous" and an "enormity"; "it is one of those players' tricks of speech" that we find "creeping into the prompt-book or into actors' parts."[2]

It is difficult, then, to go about defending Hamlet's "O's" in the face of such determined opposition. Dover Wilson's views are solidly supported by the fact that these unseemly dying groans of Hamlet have been excluded from virtually all editions of the play since Rowe (1709), the older editions based on Folio as well as the newer ones based on Quarto 2, which nevertheless include most of the other so-called Folio interpolations, as in Wilson's own edition of *Hamlet* in the New Cambridge Shakespeare (2nd edn, 1957). Critics seem to agree almost unanimously in rejecting these harsh and ineloquent "O's." After "The rest is silence," the rest has indeed been made silent for Hamlet – at least by common consent of critics and editors. If Richard Burbage liked to fatten his part with a string of catchy O-groans, we must indulge him his own histrionic eccentricities. But as for Hamlet, we cannot allow his already "too too sullied flesh" to be any further sullied in death.

Yet the O-groans keep coming at us from other parts of Shakespeare to mark moments of high passion and intense sorrow. Othello's agonized speech of self-loathing, in which he invokes all the torments of hell to punish himself for the murder of the innocent Desdemona, ends mysteriously with a quiet (but more painful because less rhetorical) sense of tragic loss: "O Desdemon! Dead Desdemon; dead. O! O!" (*Othello* 5.2.281). In the Quarto of 1622 the lines end with three "O's," a reading favored by Sisson in his *New Readings in Shakespeare*.[3] If the "O's" are already hypermetrical, it hardly matters if there are two or three of them; in other words, the line is not more or less correct metrically because it has fewer "O's." Othello's "O's" survive in most editions, while Hamlet's have disappeared, although they are analogous in dramatic and emotive function. As hypermetrical, speech-ending "O's," they are obviously vulnerable to cutting, especially in print, where metrics have a visual form.

King Lear's O-groans in the Pied Bull Quarto of 1608 have also vanished from modern editions, although in context they have a brute force appropriate for the old king's final burst of energy before he dies: "O thou wilt come no more, neuer, neuer, neuer, pray you vndo this button, thanke you sir, O, o, o, o, o" (5.3.307–8).[4] Quarto 2 (1619) has a string of five "O's" here, whereas Folio has five "never's" and no "O's." The Quarto texts suffer from what is usually diagnosed as "memorial contamination," which, like "actor's interpolation," creates a distinct impression of skulduggery on the part of the actors and/or shorthand transcribers, who had the effrontery to speak more than was set down for them in the only true copy of the play. There is a clear conflict between those who conceive the play that Shakespeare wrote as a historical document written and/or printed and those who would allow performance some status and authenticity of its own. We may ask, naively, what precisely is being contaminated and what is being coarsened by the ravages of interpolation? Not being a textual critic, I am stating the argument in a popular and nontechnical form, so that the exaggerated polarities may clarify the basic issues.

The corroborating evidence seems to indicate that Burbage used O-groans freely in performance. Was Shakespeare aware of the liberties his leading actor was taking with his text and did he warn him to cease and desist and to "speak no more than is set down" for him (*Hamlet* 3.2.41–42)? This hardly seems likely, since the two were close – perhaps daily – associates in the same theatrical enterprise and both principal sharers in the company. Apparently some of Burbage's interpolated flourishes, even the O-groans, have found their way into the best texts of Shakespeare. Did Shakespeare pick up a few hints from his leading actor, or must one postulate, as Alice Walker does for *Hamlet*,[5] that the promptbook transcripts used as printer's copy for the Folio actually include some of these tabooed actor's interpolations?

In other words, the manuscript of the play that was kept in the theater and used for performance (the "promptbook") must have been edited, as we know later theatrical promptbooks were, to account for some of the words spoken on stage that were different from what the author originally wrote. I don't mean that the promptbook was revised after every hot flash of an ad-libbing actor, but at some point significant changes which had become established in performance must have been recorded. This whole issue of performance raises special problems for editors of plays that don't exist for nondramatic texts (although public readings for such authors as Dickens, Twain, and Frost may introduce significant variants – Frost prided himself on revising his poetic texts in public).

How should we deal with changes introduced in performance? The purist would like to ignore them as obscuring the author's original intention, but a more adventurous critic would argue that these changes actualize or realize what is, at the start, merely a hypothetical, potential, and trial text. There is nothing sacrosanct about the script a playwright begins with, which he may think of as a blueprint for performance. In the nature of the medium, there can be no final, perfect, fully authentic version of a dramatic manuscript. The Platonic idea of the play must have a slightly different manifestation at each performance, so that any playtext we choose to print represents a strong compromise between the written and the spoken word, as well as an account of nonverbal action and scene-setting. One would think, as a matter of historical documentation and vitality, that editors of Shakespeare would be eager to include as many indications of contemporary performance as they could substantiate.

We know that Burbage was particularly remembered for his powerful death scenes, in which the O-groans are only one small detail. An anonymous funeral elegy on the death of Burbage on March 13, 1618, makes a metaphysical conceit out of the actor's ability to counterfeit death so convincingly:

> Oft haue I seene him, play this part in ieast,
> Soe liuly, that Spectators, and the rest
> Of his sad Crew, whilst he but seem'd to bleed,
> Amazed, thought euen then hee dyed in deed . . .[6]

Beaumont must surely be thinking specifically of Burbage when, in *The Knight of the Burning Pestle* (1607), he has Rafe die with a high-flown parody of tragic sentiments: "I die, flie, flie my soule to *Grocers* Hall. Oh, oh, oh, &c" (5.327).[7] The final "et cetera" allows for an infinite regress of O-groans to suit the histrionic occasion.

To return to the Shakespearean context, "O" was also used to indicate a sigh. There is in fact no notation to distinguish between sighs and groans; in the stage action a groan is presumably a more radical and profound expression of emotion than a sigh. In Elizabethan physiology, sighs and groans were thought to draw blood from the heart and thereby shorten human life. Ophelia describes the lovelorn Hamlet who appears to her while she is sewing in her closet as raising "a sigh so piteous and profound / As it did seem to shatter all his bulk / And end his being" (2.1.94–96), and Claudius speaks of "a spendthrift sigh, / That hurts by easing" (4.7.122–23). These examples suggest that a sigh was thought of as painful. It was not an exhalation of air associated with sentimental longing, as it is today.

Lady Macbeth's O-sighs in the Sleepwalking Scene are a powerful expression of guilt: "Here's the smell of the blood still. All the perfumes of Arabia will not sweeten this little hand. Oh, oh, oh!" (*Macbeth* 5.1.52–54). There seems to be a rhetorical and/or histrionic assumption that the O-sighs or O-groans belong at the end of a speech, as if to give it a special emotional emphasis and extension beyond the iambic pentameter line. The Doctor underscores Lady Macbeth's perturbation of mind: "What a sigh is there! The heart is sorely charged" (5.1.55–56). "Charged" means "overfull," as if the sighs were meant to relieve an acute congestion of the heart, and the Waiting Gentlewoman aptly comments: "I would not have such a heart in my bosom for the dignity of the whole body" (5.1.57–58). There is an almost exactly analogous passage about the physiology of sighing in the Seduction Scene of *A Woman Killed with Kindness* (1603) by Thomas Heywood:

> ANNE. O Master Wendoll, O.
> WENDOLL.   Sigh not, sweet saint,
>   For every sigh you breathe draws from my heart
>   A drop of blood.[8]   (VI.152–54)

Presumably actors would know how to render "O" in a style appropriate to the context. It is some sort of wistful sigh or pathetic groan, but never in performance the meaningless expletive it appears to be on the printed page. The eye tends to skip over aural signs that could be memorable on stage.

"O" is an emotive word in Shakespeare and his fellow

dramatists, and the frenzied guilt of Lady Macbeth can be matched in other scenes of distraction. In the hysterical Fly Scene of *Titus Andronicus*, Titus bursts into piercing, declamatory "O's" at his brother's attempt at comfort:

> MARCUS. Pardon me, sir; it was a black ill-favored fly,
>   Like to the Empress' Moor. Therefore I killed him.
> TITUS. O, O, O,
>   Then pardon me for reprehending thee,
>   For thou hast done a charitable deed.   (3.2.66–70)

Titus' "O's" offer the actor a good chance to express himself in the mad style. They are, in practice, open, ad-lib words, more or less insignificant and meaningless in the text, but full of emotional possibilities for the actor. Considering the frequency and wide range of "O's" in Elizabethan playtexts, we must assume that there were certain conventions about how the "O's" were to be rendered.

To literalize what we have been talking about, "O" can also be used to express pain. Falstaff's reaction to the test of his chastity is completely natural and unpremeditated:

> QUICKLY. With the trial-fire touch me his finger end.
> If he be chaste, the flame will back descend
> And turn him to no pain; but if he start
> It is the flesh of a corrupted heart.
> PISTOL. A trial, come.
> EVANS.   Come, will this wood take fire?
> *They put the tapers to his fingers, and he starts.*
> FALSTAFF. O, O, O!
>   (*The Merry Wives of Windsor* 5.5.86–91)

Falstaff's O-groans mark the end of his test and provide an unambiguous answer to his interlocutors. Here, too, the rest is silence.

It shouldn't surprise us that Burbage would want to exploit the gamut of sound effects that could be produced with a string of "O's," and we have no idea how many of his best "O's" never found their way into play manuscripts, promptbooks, or printed texts. The "O's" are only one among many ways of conveying strong feelings in a highly stylized form. The most casual reading of Elizabethan and Jacobean playtexts keeps turning up O-groans and O-sighs and O-howls for those seeking them. Here we are chiefly concerned with "O's" in series of two or more. The abundance of examples confirms the status of "O" as an expected, regular, standardized, and not at all unusual or remarkable actor's exclamation or noise/signifier for pain, grief, and heightened passion, often associated with dying.[9]

There is a telling example in Middleton and Rowley's *The Changeling* (1622). Beatrice has been mortally wounded by De Flores, and we hear her and her paramour "*within*," as an offstage chorus to the public clarifications of her father, Vermandero. Beatrice's exclamation, "Oh, oh, oh!" (5.3.139),[10] represents reality finally breaking in on the stolid and complacent Vermandero, who doesn't seem to hear his daughter until the second outcry: "Oh, oh!" (140). The father finally reacts with: "What horrid sounds are these?" (141). "Horrid" is an extremely strong word in Elizabethan usage, with its Latin sense of "horrifying," "causing horror," rather than the modern comic sense of cute but unacceptable childish behavior. At this climactic moment De Flores enters with the wounded Beatrice. Her five "O's" are a sufficient indication, at a point when the resolution must move swiftly, that Beatrice is dying.

Similarly, in *The Revenger's Tragedy* (1606) the wounded Lussurioso peppers his dying discourse with O-groans (there are 7 between 5.3.58 and 79 in the Revels edition). Spurio alerts us to the beginning of the sequence by asking, "Whose groan was that?" (49),[11] and as Vindice reveals that he has murdered Lussurioso and his father too, Lussurioso can only answer with "O's" (79). What seems on the printed page to be a failure of eloquence on the part of a dramatist who was rarely at a loss for words, must, in performance, have appeared quite adequate for the emotional needs of the occasion.

In Ford's *'Tis Pity She's a Whore* (1632), the beautifully lyrical Annabella dies with Shakespearean repetitions, and her very last sounds are hypermetrical "O's" like Hamlet's:

Forgive him [her brother, murderer, and lover Giovanni],
  Heaven – and me my sins; farewell.
Brother unkind, unkind! – Mercy, great Heaven – O! – O! – . . . .
                                    (5.3.92–93)[12]

The "O's" give the impression of suspended discourse rather than
of a speech that has been completed. In this love tragedy, they also
convey a sense of puzzled rapture and ecstasy, when the soul leaves
the body to unite with the object of contemplation (as in the long
tradition of Petrarchan and religious eroticism).[13]

Aside from Falstaff's "O's", the other examples we have
considered – Hamlet, King Lear, Othello, Lady Macbeth, Titus
Andronicus, Anne Frankford, Beatrice-Joanna, Lussurioso, and
Annabella – are all part of a meaningful system of emotional
expression in the tragedies of Shakespeare and his fellow
dramatists. To accept some of these examples, especially those
that are not hypermetrical and cannot easily be discarded, and
reject others as the grotesque and unseemly interpolations of
actors, seems to me an arbitrary and capricious way of dealing
with Elizabethan-Jacobean playtexts. It is apparent that strong
value judgments lie behind these seemingly objective textual
decisions. The anti-theatrical prejudice of this kind of criticism
may be illustrated from Harold Jenkins's precisely argued essay,
"Playhouse Interpolations in the Folio Text of *Hamlet*," although
the argument also strongly pervades Jenkins's New Arden edition
of the play (1982). It is distressing to find Jenkins constantly
covering his tracks by giving theatrical reasons for choices that
show an open contempt for the play in performance. All of what
he identifies as playhouse interpolations are, of course, playhouse
corruptions that cheapen and coarsen Shakespeare's true text.

Jenkins's remarks on Hamlet's "Mother, Mother, Mother!"
(3.4.6), spoken offstage at the beginning of the Closet Scene (and
recorded only in Folio and Quarto 1), are entirely typical:

> I infer that Q omits it because it was not in Shakespeare's
> manuscript and that the actors put it in. Indeed this is the sort of
> literalism in production from which we sometimes suffer in the
> modern theatre, as though we are not capable of imagining that

the characters in their world of the play may see or hear things that are not made visible or audible to us. Such things are at best superfluous and at worst merely crude. What sort of prince is this who cannot come to his mother's chamber without announcing his arrival by calling "Mother" three times in the corridor? It is a small thing, but it degrades the play for a moment . . . .[14]

Hamlet's O-groans are an example of the extra dialogue with which the Folio text unnecessarily embellishes the stage business, a superfluity that cheapens Shakespeare's text. Jenkins fulminates against these "inane repetitions" (p. 38) in strongly moralistic tones and with a polemical vigor unusual in scholarly discussions. "All these things, no less than the dying groans, should be recognised for the stage accretions that they are. As such they have no claim to be admitted into an edition of *Hamlet* which aims at fidelity to its author" (p. 42).

Without indulging in a point-for-point reply to Jenkins, I share the dismay expressed by Terence Hawkes at the implications of this kind of textual criticism. In his witty exposition of T. S. Eliot's line, "O, O, O, O That Shakespeherian Rag," Hawkes asks Jenkins some embarrassing questions:

Terms as confident in their presuppositions as "intrusive matter," "actor's interpolations," "stage accretions" deriving from "corruption through performance" remain the common coin of one kind of Shakespearian criticism.

But "intrusive" *into* what? "accretions" *onto* what? "corruptions" *of* what? There is no pristine manuscript of any of Shakespeare's plays. And if there were, on what basis would we grant it stronger authority, say, than the text of a prompt-book which relates, with some immediacy, to an actual contemporary performance in which the author's acquiescence was not improbable?[15]

One cannot help feeling that the argument lies well outside the limited precincts of textual criticism, and that Jenkins's distaste for the coarsening and cheapening effect of *Hamlet* in performance echoes Alexander Pope's supercilious observations about Shakespeare's actors in the preface to his edition of the plays (1725):

> Having been forced to say so much of the Players, I think I ought in justice to remark, that the Judgment, as well as Condition, of that class of people was then far inferior to what it is in our days. As then the best Playhouses were Inns and Taverns (the *Globe*, the *Hope*, the *Red Bull*, the *Fortune*, &c.), so the top of the profession were then meer Players, not Gentlemen of the stage: They were led into the Buttery by the Steward, not plac'd at the Lord's table, or Lady's toilette: and consequently were intirely depriv'd of those advantages they now enjoy, in the familiar conversation of our Nobility, and an intimacy (not to say dearness) with people of the first condition.[16]

I don't mean to exaggerate the fierceness of my own conviction that Hamlet's O-groans must immediately be restored to any genuine edition of the play. The Quarto 2 and the Folio versions obviously represent two different *Hamlets* that cannot comfortably be conflated into a single, hypothetical text. I would not even question the assumption that Quarto 2 is closer to Shakespeare's manuscript and his original intentions, while Folio reflects the theatrical history of the play during a period of about twenty years. Plays grow and develop and are not immutable. I am not trying to construct a definitive textual argument to guide future editors, but am merely trying to sketch some of the problems raised by the O-groans and by playtexts in general. I have been implying, with more or less obviousness, that opinions about the O-groans seem to depend on what moves us in the theater, on how we define dramatic poetry, and on the way we conceive Hamlet as a dramatic character.

The O-groans are painful, not mellifluous, and this applies equally to Hamlet, King Lear, Othello, Lady Macbeth, Titus Andronicus, and Falstaff. They are cries of anguish and perturbation. When rendered effectively on stage, they are disturbing without being quotable and belong naturally with the uncelebrated eloquence of Shakespeare's "unpoetic poetry."[17] The argument

over Hamlet's O-groans forces us to reconsider what is the
authentic text of Shakespeare and by what assumptions we edit
that text to suit our own preconceptions. Jenkins sees his editorial
mission as "fidelity" to his author, but unfortunately the fidelity is
to a hypothetical construct of the Author. By the workings of
bardolatry, Jenkins wants to protect his Shakespeare from the
interpolations, accretions, and other ravages that the base actors
have forced upon him. His purpose is really to purify Shakespeare
and especially *Hamlet*. In this endeavor, it seems to make a great
deal of difference whether we like our Hamlet and our Shakespeare
rough or smooth, and whether we insist with Pope that the
audiences in the theater be "people of the first condition."

PART II
—
THE ORGANIZATION AND DISPOSITION OF DRAMATIC ENERGIES

5

Analogy and infinite regress

"Infinite regress" has become a fashionable term for explaining why narratives do not move forward in a straight line, but tend to move sideways in ragged ellipses. The term is especially applicable to Shakespeare and the episodic nature of Elizabethan drama. The danger of moving forward in a straight line is that you will come to the end too quickly, and the end is usually the most difficult and least satisfying part of the structure. One function of infinite regress, then, is to avoid the ending or at least to keep it at a distance for as long as possible. Regression is the opposite of going forward, and it offers a way of enriching the narrative by repetition, echoing, mirroring, duplication (with its hint of duplicity), displacement, or whatever idea satisfies the need for an effective redeployment of the same or related materials in an analogical relationship. Instead of going forward, the narrative keeps moving back and forth. As readers or audience we are not allowed to get a firm purchase on the narrative; we are not supposed to be too comfortable in knowing where we're at or where we're going. But regression is in itself a movement as definite as progression.

French critics have used the heraldic term, *mise en abyme*, from Gide's *Journal*,[1] to refer to the same narrative perspective as infinite regress. It is the microcosmic image of a heraldic shield that reduplicates in miniature the larger shield. It is the play within the play – and Gide specifically mentions *Hamlet* – the mirror in a Dutch or Flemish painting that shows us the scene of the painting, the Russian dolls within dolls, the Quaker on the Quaker Oats box who is depicted holding a box of Quaker Oats on which another

Quaker is mirrored holding another box of Quaker Oats in a visual regress that winds down in an ever-diminishing infinity. *Mise en abyme* implies a series of reflected images that is systematically reduced by the laws of perspective. There is an element of optical trickery in infinite regress, since we can never theoretically reach the end no matter how much the image may be attenuated in its progress from foreground to background. We can only end by an imaginative leap out of the *mise en abyme* assumptions and the infinite regress pattern. We must abandon mutual reflections or self-reflexiveness and choose the ending by an act of will.

Hamlet fits well with this kind of thinking because its narrative is so discontinuous. What is usually called delay in pursuing revenge can be seen as an effect of imaginative displacement. Hamlet is in good company among revengers both on the stage and off in thinking of revenge as a work of art. Like sexual fulfillment, revenge must be perfected. Its foreplay is dramatically conceived, and there must be a fitting relation between preparation and execution. It is no revenge at all merely to butcher your antagonist. Revenge plays as a genre lend themselves to infinite regress patterns, since the ending is by its nature anticlimactic. All the excitement is in the process. It should come as no surprise that the revenge theme analogizes so well with two kinds of play: sexual play and the play in the theater. It has long been recognized that the plotter in the play functions as a surrogate dramatist, but the seducer or sexual plotter is also devising and enacting a scenario that will lead to its own triumphant conclusion. Triumphant but disappointing, since both orgasm and murder have a finality that eludes any further inventiveness. There is a disproportionate ratio of means to end, so that, in retrospect, the elaborateness and the artifice seem like ends in themselves without any reference to ulterior fulfillments.

Hamlet's fiction and dream of passion strangely confound bloody and unnatural thoughts, murder and incest, lasciviousness and aggression. He is wallowing in the "rank sweat of an enseamèd bed" (3.4.93) at the very moment that we expect his thoughts to be "bloody, or be nothing worth" (4.4.66). The fact that Claudius and Gertrude function as double antagonists – at least in Hamlet's mind – tends to fractionate his revenge and to make an analogizing, mirroring habit of mind almost a necessity. Hamlet's ability to transform his preoccupations as the occasion demands – to displace them or "regress" them, as we might say – allows him to give his revenge a much fuller imaginative scope. He creates a series of fictions to expatiate on the revenge theme, both to express the need for revenge and to prevent the revenge from actually taking place.

The first statement of the infinite regress theme is in Claudius' smooth speech about mourning. The death of Hamlet's father – not yet murder to the audience on stage and off but only death – is nature's "common theme," "who still hath cried, / From the first corse till he that died today, / 'This must be so' " (1.2.103–6). It is a self-justifying series, the common fate – "all that lives must die, / Passing through nature to eternity" (72–73) – so that the Queen may justifiably needle her son's "obstinate condolement": "Why seems it [death] so particular with thee?" (75). "Particular" vs. "common": In the infinite regression the particular is swallowed up in the common. As Claudius puts it (in the Polonius style of excessive specification): "But you must know your father lost a father, / That father lost, lost his" (89–90). The particular grief is trivialized in the network of analogy, and the mourner is bound only "In filial obligation for some term / To do obsequious sorrow" (91–92). This is a formal and limited regress by which personal sorrow is ritualistically – and perhaps also bureaucratically – minimized.

But in his first appearance Hamlet bridles at this formulaic interpretation of mourning. He cannot lose himself in "forms, moods, shapes of grief," his "inky cloak," his "customary suits of solemn black," his "windy suspiration of forced breath," "the fruitful river in the eye," and "the dejected havior of the visage" (1.2.77–82). There is an excessive specification of negatives because the signs of grief are merely the counterfeit presentment of inner feelings:

> These indeed seem,
> For they are actions that a man might play,

But I have that within which passes show;
These but the trappings and the suits of woe.
(1.2.83–86)

It is important that Hamlet in his first encounter with the King makes such a strong distinction between external and internal, the world of outer appearances and shapes and the world of bitter, inner realities. The whole play turns on Claudius' almost successful manipulation of those appearances, the "forgèd process" by which, as the Ghost explains, the "whole ear of Denmark" is "Rankly abused" (1.5.36–38). This initial contrast between inner truth and outer deception, between public professions and private anguish, establishes the necessity for Hamlet to protect himself against the reality of Claudius and his court. Hamlet's imaginative scenarios displace and replace the official version of truth that is "given out" (1.5.35) in Denmark.

By the time the traveling Players arrive on the scene, Hamlet is already well along in preparing his role as revenger. It is important to remember that this is conceived as a stage part in relation to other stage revengers. Coleridge and the Romantic critics were right about Hamlet in so far as they understood the tremendous transformation Hamlet undergoes because of the Ghost's revelations. Not that Hamlet is ever a sensitive intellectual incapable of action – he can run Polonius through behind the arras and delight in the nice irony by which Rosencrantz and Guildenstern "go to't" (5.2.56), "it" being their deaths in England. But revenge raises special problems that go beyond the "virtù" and manliness required of a Renaissance prince. Laertes is a natural revenger, ready to cut Hamlet's "throat i' th' church" (4.7.126), and the rugged Pyrrhus, all "Roasted in wrath and fire" and "o'ersizèd with coagulate gore" (2.2.472–73), relentlessly stalks the aged Priam and slaughters him with inhuman, mechanical ferocity. But Hamlet is different. He is no natural swordsman like Tybalt in *Romeo and Juliet*, nor even a natural swaggerer like Laertes or Pistol (in the two parts of *Henry IV*).

Hamlet's revenge is played out in revenge fantasy, by which he enacts a series of roles that do not come easily to him. By the workings of infinite regress, Hamlet sets life and art against each other as he tries to find out what it feels like to be a revenger. This experimentation gives the play a histrionic cast, since Hamlet is not only playing the revenger, but also the mad, malcontent, dispossessed prince. All the guises are mutually illuminating. Hamlet is also a jilted lover – the shrewd Polonius stakes his reputation on the authenticity of this role – and Hamlet's frustration and sexual nausea are certainly as acute as Ophelia's. If we take all these possible roles into account, we see a Hamlet radically different from any other character in the play. In order to realize his part, he must necessarily be full of plots, disguises, displacements, and fantastications. He literally has "that within which passes show" (1.2.85). He seems to have the capacity to create his own play.

The Player's intensely felt declamation about Pyrrhus' murder of Priam and the climactic events of the fall of Troy make a strong impression on Hamlet, who finds poetry and drama a more satisfying emotional outlet than real life. By being displaced, the events in a play-within-a-play allow for a more direct and permissible response, so that it is through observing his own powerful reactions to the Dido and Aeneas play that Hamlet comes to understand the power of a fiction "to catch the conscience of the King" (2.2.617). The play is part of an imagined world that is truer and more convincing than the sordid world of actual fact: "No, no, they do but jest, poison in jest; no offense i' th' world" (3.2.240–41). Hamlet's triumph in the Play Scene is a histrionic and imaginative triumph; it is not surprising that immediately afterwards the events of the real world move so quickly and so decisively against him.

The old truism about Hamlet's delay is no longer viable because he doesn't literally delay at all. The Ghost's "fat weed / That roots [or "rots" in Folio] itself in ease on Lethe wharf" (1.5.32–33) has no relation at all to Hamlet, whom revenge churns into a frenzy of imagination and activity. The revenge is not delayed but elaborately reasoned, moralized, and pictured. Hamlet is so full of so many different kinds of revenge – so many "deep plots" (5.2.9) – that he has no specific plan of action at all. He is totally unlike

Laertes and Claudius in Act IV, Scene vii, as they coolly and
prudently devise the triple plot by which Hamlet cannot choose
but fall. Here we have real revengers at work, and we admire the
intense practicality with which Claudius proposes "a back or
second" (4.7.153) if the envenomed rapier plot backfires – as it
does. Hamlet never conceives revenge in these terms because he is
trapped in an infinite regress. Each imagined scene or scenario
conjures up another that is superior to it, so that none at all can
possibly achieve its objective. It is like the fantasy of the
masturbator that Taylor Stoehr speaks of so eloquently in
"Pornography, Masturbation, and the Novel": the act is so
satisfying in itself that gratification can only signify an end to
pleasure.[2] Unlike Claudius and Laertes in Act IV, Scene vii,
Hamlet's vengeful thoughts are an object of contemplation in
themselves. They more than gratify his inflamed desire for
revenge, whereas actual murder at this point would only be
unsatisfying and anticlimactic.

The self-reflexive mood of infinite regress is amply illustrated
in Hamlet's "rogue and peasant slave" soliloquy at the end of Act
II, Scene ii, as he switches irritably between the perspectives of
literature and life. He begins by upbraiding himself for not being
up to the fictive passions of the Player, who is so moved by his own
performance that he breaks down in real tears at the sorrows of
Hecuba, "a clout upon that head / Where late the diadem stood"
(2.2.517–18). The Player's visage has "wanned," he has "Tears in
his eyes, distraction in his aspect, / A broken voice, and his whole
function suiting / With forms to his conceit" (564–67). But these,
of course, are "actions that a man might play" (1.2.84); they are
the "forms, moods, shapes of grief" (82). We are back at the
infinite regress paradox. Does the Player, not as an actor but as a
private person, genuinely feel for Hecuba? We have no way of
knowing, since his only identity is as the Player, although Tom
Stoppard teases the paradox in *Rosencrantz and Guildenstern Are
Dead*. In what sense is it "monstrous" that the Player should be able
to "force his soul so to his own conceit" (2.2.561, 563)? Why is it
"monstrous" to act "in a fiction, in a dream of passion" (562)? This
is Hamlet's central problem as a revenger: he cannot gauge his

own sincerity, he cannot move easily and convincingly from literature to life, he cannot allow the two worlds to merge, but must strenuously insist that they are mirror images of each other.

Hecuba is a Gertrude analogue, since her "loins" are "lank and all o'erteemèd" (2.2.519), and at Hamlet's mother's age "The heyday in the blood is tame, it's humble, / And waits upon the judgment" (3.4.70–71). But Hamlet also imagines, with adolescent ardor, that his mother is a rampant sexual being, "honeying and making love / Over the nasty sty" (94–95). There is a glaring Oedipal inconsistency here. In this respect, Hecuba seems more a grandmotherly analogue to Gertrude (as Priam is a grandfatherly analogue to old Hamlet), so that Hamlet can speculate how the Player would react if he had a Gertrude and not a Hecuba as "the motive and the cue for passion" (2.2.571). If the Player "would drown the stage with tears / And cleave the general ear with horrid speech" (573–74), what then should Hamlet do? In the mirror of infinite regress, Hamlet's hypothetical reactions are escalated to unseemly rant. The hyperboles – "Make mad the guilty and appall the free, / Confound the ignorant, and amaze indeed / The very faculties of eyes and ears" (574–76) – literally "tear a passion to tatters, to very rags" (3.1.10) and "out-herod Herod" (14–15). They violate all of Hamlet's worthy precepts to the Players at the beginning of Act III. Why does Hamlet indulge in such bombastic rhetoric in his "rogue and peasant slave" soliloquy? This is acting at its worst, and it ends with a grandiloquent period in the style of King Cambyses: "Bloody, bawdy villain! / Remorseless, treacherous, lecherous, kindless villain! / O, vengeance!" (2.2.591–93). Isn't Hamlet aware of how ridiculous he sounds?

Of course he is, and the next lines are an apology for ranting. He is unpacking his "heart with words"; he is "a-cursing like a very drab, / A scullion!" (as in Folio) (2.2.598–99). He began by wanting to outdo the Player in passion and sincerity, but his attempt proves a dismal failure. He is no Player, although he certainly tried to sound like one. His revenge keeps being displaced onto better and more efficacious speeches. Should he be histrionic or natural? Is he acting from the truth or from "a fiction," "a dream of passion" (562)? None of these questions is answerable, but the interrogative mode establishes the tone of the soliloquy. At the end, Hamlet returns to the world of the play, "the very cunning of the scene" (602), that will trap the unwary spectator into guilty confession. Hamlet is the histrionic doctor who will "tent" or probe his uncle/father "to the quick" (609), as in the Prayer Scene Dr Hamlet prescribes for the praying King: "This physic but prolongs thy sickly days" (3.3.96). Revenge is a mystery. We keep being shunted from the play world to the real world and back again without any conclusive certainty. Hamlet's revenge seems to slip away into a distant time warp as he tries out various scenarios of his own invention.

The Play Scene is Hamlet's big moment, where literature and life come together and he can function as commentator, sophisticated court wit (in the style of the aristocratic audience of *Love's Labor's Lost*), master of ceremonies, and secret author. *The Mousetrap* has a specific purpose: to "unkennel" the King's "occulted guilt" (3.1.82–83), and Hamlet and Horatio have concerted their efforts as literary critics/detectives. The play world becomes the real world, "the image of a murder done in Vienna" (3.2.244), while the real world of Claudius and his court is fictive in the most literal sense of presenting false appearances of virtue and harmony. The fiction is the cover-up; the reality is the secret murder now being re-enacted in the seeming fiction of Gonzago: "The story is extant, and written in very choice Italian" (3.2.268–69). The mirroring regress is obvious but effective, as we get caught up in the illusion of the play within the play that seems to guarantee the authenticity of the real play that is not a play at all.

In his licensed role as presenter, Hamlet assumes a lewd camaraderie with Ophelia, who cannot protest openly on this public occasion. Hamlet's "country matters" (3.2.119) are presumably accompanied by country manners as the mad and witty Prince insults the fair Ophelia. She can do nothing to ward off his sexual assault, which craftily substitutes verbal aggression for any attempt at lovemaking. "That's a fair thought to lie between maids' legs" (121–22) – not a thought that leads to acts, but only a hot thought that replaces hot deeds. As Paris says satirically of Troilus, "hot blood begets hot thoughts, and hot thoughts beget hot deeds, and hot deeds is love" (*Troilus and Cressida* 3.1.128–29). The Play Scene in *Hamlet* recapitulates the Nunnery Scene immediately preceding, where Hamlet lasciviously upbraids Ophelia for being a woman and therefore the tempter and corrupter of men. There is no basis at all, except in Hamlet's lewd imaginings, for thinking of Ophelia as either overdressed or heavily made up, as jigging and ambling, as lisping and making her wantonness her ignorance (3.1.145–48). This is all in Hamlet's mind, so that his sexual assault is not only entirely unjustified, it is merely a projection of his own frustrated and turbulent fantasy. Like the murder to which revenge is prompting, sex is the logical enactment of the guilty scenarios that trouble Hamlet's mind. But he avoids fulfillments, both in murder and in sex, because gratification would immediately signal an end to fantasy. The end is even more disturbing than the fantasy, which can at least be played out and controlled.

Hamlet's failure to kill Claudius in the Prayer Scene has been much criticized by bloodthirsty critics, who want to see their hero get on with it. I find this kind of thinking very surprising, as if the criteria for revenge and murder in literature were different from those in life. We are sure at this point that Hamlet will not kill Claudius even though he has an excellent opportunity to do so because, on the infinite regress assumptions, no opportunity is good enough. The King is praying, and even though it is abundantly clear from what Claudius says that his prayer is a hollow sham, Hamlet has better scenarios in mind:

> When he is drunk asleep, or in his rage,
> Or in th' incestuous pleasure of his bed,
> At game a-swearing, or about some act
> That has no relish of salvation in't . . . .
> (3.3.89–92)

Hamlet is alarmingly visual, especially in his voyeuristic recreation of the primal scene: that incestuous bed much preoccupies him in the following scene with his mother. It is interesting that the scenarios projected by Hamlet have no relation to the actual murder of Claudius in Act V, Scene ii. They are all part of Hamlet's guilty image-making, by which he is trying to order, both aggressively and sexually, a recalcitrant reality that eludes his control. No scenario is good enough because the murder of Claudius is still an unrealizable fantasy, and Hamlet is preoccupied with his own fictions.

The Closet Scene with Gertrude grows directly out of the Prayer Scene with Claudius: two parallel encounters with a false father/uncle (no dialogue) and a mock mother (much dialogue). In the Closet Scene Hamlet's guilty sexual imaginings are even more repulsive than in the scenes with Ophelia. He makes sex the vehicle for everything that is "rank and gross" in the unweeded garden of the world (1.2.135–36) and in this sense anticipates the violent sexual nausea of King Lear:

> But to the girdle do the gods inherit,
> Beneath is all the fiend's.
> There's hell, there's darkness, there is the sulphurous pit,
> Burning, scalding, stench, consumption; fie, fie, fie!
> pah, pah!
>
> (*King Lear* 4.6.128–32)

Hamlet imagines sexual scenes for his mother with her new lover that arise out of his own febrile eroticism: "Let the bloat King tempt you again to bed, / Pinch wanton on your cheek, call you his mouse" (3.4.183–84). We recognize Hamlet's own inflamed incestuous longings in this speech, where sex is spicy, forbidden, and tantalizingly dirty. He wants his uncle/father and his mother to enact his own worst thoughts, so that they can relieve him of the unbearable pressures of his own mind. The "reechy" or smoky/greasy kisses and the king "paddling in your neck with his damned fingers" (185–86) are shocking details, like the best sexual fiction, where the imagination must do yeoman's service for the deed. But Claudius and Gertrude are no Antony and Cleopatra, which is precisely the ironic point of Hamlet's sexual commentary. If what Hamlet says were literally represented on stage, we obviously wouldn't need Hamlet to tell us about it. Like

Troilus' spying on Cressida in the Greek camp (*Troilus and Cressida* V,ii), Hamlet's mirroring perspectives raise a sexual regress parallel to the revenge regress. Both function as autonomous imaginative systems that feed upon themselves without any hope of resolution.

The culmination of Hamlet's revenge thinking comes in the "How all occasions do inform against me" soliloquy in Act IV, Scene iv. Practical critics have pointed out how preposterous Hamlet's thinking is at this point, especially when he says:

> I do not know
> Why yet I live to say, "This thing's to do,"
> Sith I have cause, and will, and strength, and means
> To do't. (4.4.43–46)

This is surely an odd declaration from a man who is a prisoner under guard being shipped off against his will to England. But it concludes the extravagantly circular and self-fulfilling thoughts of Hamlet's revenge. Fortinbras and his army have an analogous function to the Player's speech about Hecuba in the "rogue and peasant slave" soliloquy (II,ii). In both, Hamlet freely analogizes himself with a powerful example, which is then invidiously compared to himself. The comparison is clearly laid out: if Fortinbras for the sake of his own honor can find pretext for a quarrel in a straw, what then should Hamlet do, who has a real quarrel, "a father killed, a mother stained, / Excitements of my reason and my blood" (4.4.57–58)? Should he "cleave the general ear with horrid speech, / Make mad the guilty and appall the free" (2.2.573–74)? The declamatory ending of the later soliloquy certainly reminds us of the earlier rant: "O, from this time forth, / My thoughts be bloody, or be nothing worth!" (4.4.65–66).

But, we must object, Hamlet's thoughts have always been bloody enough; he has never had a problem in that area. Why should his thoughts be especially bloody at this point, when there is virtually no opportunity to put them into action? Thus, even when he is exhorting himself with a ringing couplet, he still seems to be preoccupied with bloody thoughts and not bloody deeds. In contrast to Hamlet, the impetuous warrior Fortinbras seems to have no thoughts at all, and he is excluded from the conversation in this scene. His cynical Captain speaks for him.

The infinite regress patterns of revenge and sexuality trap Hamlet in a circle of bloody and bawdy thoughts that can have no resolution. By definition, it is a self-contained and self-reflexive system that has no legitimate end because the system is a defense against endings and always returns upon itself. There is, however, a way out, what Stoehr calls "the leap":

> It is not something which the hero can accomplish as an exploit, or the author as a tour de force; it is achieved only by "letting up," by an act of faith that the other is there, and need not be proved or attained.[3]

Although this was written specifically about gothic and porno-graphic fiction, its folklore pattern applies surprisingly well to the structure of *Hamlet*.

The structural "leap" in *Hamlet* occurs when he providentially escapes his plotted death in England and returns from the sea voyage. This represents a sharp break in the action that delivers us from the circularities of infinite regress. We feel that Hamlet's perspective has changed and he is no longer the revenger of the narrative preceding the sea voyage. Suddenly he recognizes that his "deep plots do pall" (5.2.9) and that "There's a divinity that shapes our ends, / Rough-hew them how we will" (10–11). In other words, he sees in his escape proof that heaven is "ordinant" (48), down to the last detail of his "father's signet" which he has in his purse. He escapes not through plotting but through "rashness" (7), a spontaneous, spur-of-the-moment good luck that never deserts him. He can now with good conscience place himself in the hands of Providence and trust in the special omniscience that governs the fall of the sparrow (220–21). Everything in the last scene falls into place with magical swiftness and efficacy, although Hamlet himself dies in the general slaughter that brings down Claudius, Gertrude, and Laertes. There is no escaping the death that Hamlet has so vividly imagined.

Hamlet's speculations about death in Act V are an infinite regress series that leads him out of the labyrinth of revenge in which he was mazed earlier in the play. He finally accepts the inevitability of death, "The undiscovered country, from whose bourn / No traveler returns" (3.1.79–80), and especially his own death. He also accepts his own "tainted mind"; the Ghost's imperative, "Taint not thy mind" (1.5.85), has no potency to free Hamlet from the higher imperatives of revenge. His "readiness" (5.2.223) is pre-eminently a readiness to die, and this is the recognition of the "other," the "leap," that takes him out of the circle in which he has been moving. By putting himself in the hands of Providence, he finally accepts the ending, both of the play and of himself. The final scene in the graveyard recalls the earlier mourning sequence with Claudius – "your father lost a father, / That father lost, lost his" (1.2.89–90) – and also Hamlet's scene of burlesque jesting about the body of Polonius, where the mad prince expatiates on "how a king may go a progress through the guts of a beggar" (4.3.30–31).

This transformational thinking is much altered in the Graveyard Scene, where Hamlet postulates a series of satirical character sketches for the bones the gravedigger is uncovering: "This might be the pate of a politician" (5.1.79), "Or of a courtier" (83), or "a lawyer" (100). The sequence continues with Yorick, the court jester, "a fellow of infinite jest, of most excellent fancy" (186–87). Hamlet's meditation on the skull of Yorick also nauseates him: "My gorge rises at it" (189). The mixture of physical disgust with unbounded affection and nostalgia gives this scene an unforgettable poignancy: "Here hung those lips that I have kissed I know not how oft" (189–91).

The death sequence ends with wild imaginings about Alexander the Great, whose "noble dust" Hamlet traces in the conceited style of Richard II, until he finds it "stopping a bunghole" (205–6) of a beer barrel. Hamlet shows himself to be a fellow of infinite jest as he ends his infinite regress on the noble and ignoble dead with "Imperious Caesar, dead and turned to clay," who "Might stop a hole to keep the wind away" (215–16). This is the "Imperious Caesar" of the tragedy that was presented shortly before *Hamlet* in the Lord Chamberlain's Men's repertory, and in which, metadramatically, Polonius "did enact Julius Caesar. I was killed i' th' Capitol; Brutus killed me" (3.2.105–6). These somber and frivolous speculations about death color all of Act V and explain why Hamlet feels "how ill all's here about my heart" (5.2.213–14). He is enacting his own death, and the macabre jesting serves to master his own anxiety. Once this realization occurs, then everything else follows naturally from it. The conceptualization of death proves to be a harder task than the enactment of revenge, and, in this context, death can only have meaning if it includes revenge.

Perhaps the purest infinite regress formula is the shaggy dog story, in which, whether the dog is too shaggy or not shaggy enough, the end is teasingly and anticlimactically avoided. In Legman's monumental collection of dirty jokes (or, more properly, erotic folklore), he has an almost perfect example of the infinite regress, shaggy dog story:

> Chap goes to a brothel. Opens doors into passage, at end of which are two doors, on one of which is marked MARRIED, and on the other SINGLE. Chap chooses SINGLE, and finds himself in another passage with two doors, marked EXPERIENCED and INEXPERIENCED. Entering by the door marked INEXPERIENCED he finds himself in yet another corridor with two doors marked UNDER 5 INCHES and OVER 5 INCHES. Opening the former, he finds himself in the street.[4]

The story ends with the quester back where he started, presumably ready to begin over again. There is a subtle value system built into the choices, but the quester will always end in the street regardless of what decisions he makes. The regress pattern is infinitely negative.

But in *Hamlet* the protagonist does not end where he began. Although he dies, he manages to escape from the regressive labyrinth of his revenge. He leaps out of the regress system by asking a different set of questions and by testing the totality of the choices he had previously assumed. One answer to the system is to ignore the system, or at least the rigidly binary possibilities the system proposes. All the offerings are wrong, so that, according to the folklore pattern, it is only by the undiscovered third door that one may enter. When Hamlet returns from England he is no longer a mourner "in suits of solemn black" (1.2.78); presumably he is now wearing his "sea gown scarfed" (5.2.13) about him. He is also no longer the melancholy, lovesick revenger feigning madness. All these roles have been left behind, and, like a good actor, he is waiting to play out whatever new parts are offered him. In all senses of the term, both metaphysical and histrionic, he is ready.

The infinite regress idea, with its emphasis on analogical reasoning, projects a new Hamlet who is less a creature of will (or lack of will) than a creation of fantasy and fiction. Hamlet is in some sense both the victim and the triumphant exploiter of his own fantasy. He manages, finally, to confront his destiny with determination and stoical assurance, but he has come a long way from the witty, metaphorizing, and brilliant figure at the beginning of the action. By sacrificing the play of infinite regress, he has also sacrificed some part of his powers of speculation and intellect. As he tells Rosencrantz and Guildenstern, "O God, I could be bounded in a nutshell and count myself a king of infinite space, were it not that I have bad dreams" (2.2.258–60). There is a different wisdom in counting oneself "a king of infinite space" from placing oneself in the hands of Providence. This represents a passive wisdom that cuts off the free play of imagination which is most characteristic of Hamlet's style. If there is "special providence in the fall of a sparrow" (5.2.220–21), then Hamlet does not need to provide his own scenarios; he is part of the providential plan. This reduces his image-making, histrionic function, since he can no longer refuse any occasion that is offered, including the ill-starred fencing match, against which his foreboding heart warns him.

We feel Hamlet's tragedy most acutely in these final scenes, as he moves to fulfill a destiny in which he will be destroyed along with his enemies. We feel the pain of his certain death. He is grappling with a destiny he only partly understands, and what he understands fills him with horror. He tries to become a revenger in the old blood-and-thunder style of Laertes and Pyrrhus, but his imaginative attempt breaks down with the murder of Polonius, and he can only escape the claustrophobia of infinite regress by putting himself in the hands of Providence. At this point he is ready both to kill the king and to die himself. He is a fully tragic figure.

We sympathize so profoundly with the tragic protagonist because we are both amazed and sorrowful at his tragic fate. Hamlet's problems become our problems in the sense in which conscience and consciousness "make cowards of us all" (3.1.83). Merely by being alive we share in Hamlet's anguish. Once he conclusively moves toward his own ending and the ending of Claudius, we marvel at his decisiveness and courage. This sense of the destruction of everything worthy, of the wasting of human life and opportunity, is a tragic emotion in Shakespeare's time and in ours. Hamlet can no longer be the courtier, soldier, scholar of Ophelia's description: "Th' expectancy and rose of the fair state, / The glass of fashion, and the mold of form, / Th' observed of all observers" (3.1.155–57). He must put all that aside for aims and motives more monumental and less worthy. To see Hamlet being destroyed by fulfilling his destiny can only fill us with inexplicable horror. The pity and the mystery of it are summed up in Ophelia's moving couplet: "O, woe is me / T' have seen what I have seen, see what I see!" (3.1.163–64).

6

The exact middle of *Hamlet*

The ending of *Hamlet* is precisely marked by Hamlet's surprising return from his sea voyage to England. His escape from the execution to which Claudius is sending him is seen to be a providential act, and we feel that Hamlet is now older, wiser, and readier to cope with revenge. Before the sea voyage, however, Hamlet is moving in an entirely different direction. From his soliloquy at the end of Act III, Scene ii ("Now could I drink hot blood") through his soliloquy at the end of Act IV, Scene iv ("How all occasions do inform against me"), Hamlet tries out the role of revenger, with all of the swagger and rant connected with it. This identifies a very exact middle of the play. The beginning, the middle, and the end of *Hamlet* are unusually explicit in their demarcations.

The soliloquy at the end of the Play Scene (II,ii) marks a new resolution in Hamlet to take the revenge action justified by the *Mousetrap* play. He has indeed caught the conscience of the King, and he is now preparing himself to do battle with his enemies, as revealed by the Ghost and confirmed by the play. Although Hamlet's soliloquies have received excessive critical attention, the "Now could I drink hot blood" soliloquy has been almost entirely neglected. It is therefore worth quoting in full, if only to remind readers of its unfamiliarity and to show how different its style is from the better-known soliloquies. It is didactic and expository rather than contemplative, and it has no memorable, quotable lines – or at least not the kind of poetic lines we would like to be memorable. In the immediate context, Polonius has just exited after arranging for the interview between Hamlet and his mother (at which the old counselor will be fatally concealed), and the menacing Rosencrantz and Guildenstern follow Polonius offstage. Hamlet now has a quiet moment in which to prepare himself for the scene with his mother:

> 'Tis now the very witching time of night,
> When churchyards yawn, and hell itself breathes out
> Contagion to this world. Now could I drink hot blood
> And do such business as the bitter day[1]
> Would quake to look on. Soft, now to my mother.
> O heart, lose not thy nature; let not ever
> The soul of Nero enter this firm bosom.
> Let me be cruel, not unnatural;
> I will speak daggers to her, but use none.
> My tongue and soul in this be hypocrites:
> How in my words somever she be shent,
> To give them seals never, my soul, consent!
>
> (3.2.396–407)

In the theatrical tradition "To be, or not to be" has become Hamlet's most characteristic utterance rather than the more vigorous and heroic "Now could I drink hot blood," which plunges us right into the Hamlet world of Saxo Grammaticus and Norse saga, where the timely epic boast establishes the hero's manly claims. Hamlet is setting out to do doughty deeds, or perhaps he is just steeling himself rhetorically for his role as revenger. This new mood represents the practical consequences of Hamlet's triumph with *The Mousetrap*. The speech at the end of Act III, Scene ii begins a movement in the action that develops and intensifies in the Prayer Scene (III,iii) and the Closet Scene (III,iv) and is not completed until Hamlet's departure for England at the end of Act IV, Scene iv. The "How all occasions do inform against me" speech that closes this scene has a direct relation to the soliloquy at the end of Act III, Scene ii, and this sequence of scenes from the end of III, ii to the end of IV, iv marks a sharply defined middle movement of the play.

The structural unity of this middle sequence is almost too explicit for Shakespeare. Perhaps he felt uncomfortable about putting such a powerful emphasis on Hamlet's homicidal mood – in making him so much like Pyrrhus and Laertes and the standard revenger type – especially when this unsympathetic image of the hero is only temporary, a passing phase. When Hamlet returns from his sea voyage, he has placed himself and his revenge in the hands of Providence: "There's a divinity that shapes our ends, / Rough-hew them how we will" (5.2.10–11). These are radically different sentiments from the gruesome and diabolic promptings of the soliloquy in Act III, Scene ii. The hot blood Hamlet is speaking about is presumably the blood of a newly killed enemy, whom you humiliate beyond death by ritually drinking, still warm and bubbling – an outrage he is powerless to prevent. This is the primitive Hamlet of the sagas, boasting heroically and preparing himself for the kill. The soliloquy is permeated with talk of hell, Judgment Day ("the bitter day" of Quarto 2), bloody murder, and cruelty. The scene ends with Hamlet, sword in hand,[2] proceeding to his mother's room.

As Samuel Johnson understood so well, Hamlet's hesitations about killing Claudius are even more diabolical than his original, spontaneous impulse to take revenge. Hamlet's "more horrid hent" (3.3.88) comes from the damnable desire not only to kill the king physically, but also to destroy his soul, and, according to Johnson, these sentiments are "too horrible to be read or to be uttered."[3] Hamlet's soliloquy in the Prayer Scene continues directly from the soliloquy in Act III, Scene ii – there are, in fact, no intervening speeches by Hamlet. "Now might I do it pat" (3.3.73) seems to echo, in a lower and more colloquial tone, the menacing style of "Now could I drink hot blood" (3.2.398); and "Dead for a ducat, dead!" (3.4.25) at the murder of Polonius fits in with these swaggering exclamations. In the Prayer Scene with Claudius, Hamlet is already practicing the cruelty he has resolved on for his mother: "Let me be cruel, not unnatural" (3.2.403), and in fact thinks himself awfully clever to pass up the imperfect revenge for the much better opportunities that will soon present themselves – ones that have "no relish of salvation" (3.3.92) in them. Hamlet's exit line in the Prayer Scene – "This physic but prolongs thy sickly days" (96) – expresses a certain sadistic delight in toying with his uncle-victim. The delay in revenge is a false medicine (or "physic") which doesn't cure the patient, but only prolongs his incurable illness and therefore makes life a torment to him.

It is in this fearsome mood that we soon hear Hamlet in the Closet Scene calling wildly from offstage: "Mother, Mother, Mother!" (3.4.6). These are memorable lines for an actor to deliver, and they could, if spoken with the right mixture of bitter accusation, thwarted love, and inexpressible anguish, sum up all that has been troubling Hamlet. It is wrong to think that Gertrude overreacts to her passionate son in this scene, and that the meddlesome but extremely shrewd Polonius is killed merely because the Queen overestimates the gravity of the situation. This mollification of the scene overlooks the function of the soliloquy in Act III, Scene ii as an expository prologue. That soliloquy bears directly on the scene with Gertrude, and, as psychoanalysts have pointed out, the Closet Scene is the best example of Hamlet's revenge being displaced from his uncle – a father-surrogate – onto his mother. That is why the Ghost appears to "whet" Hamlet's "almost blunted purpose" (3.4.112) and to set him on the right track. Notice, however, that the Closet Scene continues for more than a hundred anguished lines after the Ghost's departure.

The chief function of the "Now could I drink hot blood" soliloquy is to allow Hamlet to master his overpowering impulse to matricide. Like Polonius in his moral injunctions to the departing Laertes, Hamlet presents himself with a series of imperatives: "O heart, lose not thy nature," which is to be compassionate to one's mother; "let not ever / The soul of Nero[4] enter this firm bosom" (3.2.401-2). It doesn't require any subtle psychological insight to understand that Hamlet is expressing forbidden wishes precisely in order to control them. He must bring the inexpressible to the level of consciousness in order to be able to deal with it. He is directing his conduct – even rehearsing it – in a way that is unusual in the play. "Let me be cruel, not unnatural" (403) presents false alternatives; both parts of the proposition are equally reprehensible. "Unnatural" refers, of course, to Nero and matricide, but why must Hamlet commit himself in advance to being cruel? That is one of the puzzles of the Closet Scene, which is designed more to relieve Hamlet's lacerating aggression, oedipal anxiety, fear and longing for the primal scene, and general sexual nausea than to purge Gertrude's "fighting soul" (3.4.114). The Queen's apparent reformation and spiritual conversion seem incidental to Hamlet's own outrageous self-expression.

In the "Now could I drink hot blood" soliloquy, Hamlet continues to lay before himself the moral directives that must govern the scene with his mother: "I will speak daggers to her, but use none" (3.2.404). Again, we are at the magical and preoccupying idea of murder, which terrifies and fascinates Hamlet the revenger. Remember that at this point Hamlet is convinced of the truth of the Ghost's narration, which points to Gertrude's adultery and probable complicity in the murder of old Hamlet. It is not until the Closet Scene is well under way that Hamlet seems deflected from this certainty. Gertrude's incredulous question, "As kill a king?" (3.4.31), seems to satisfy Hamlet's curiosity on that issue, and the swiftness with which the matter is settled indicates that the technical guilt or innocence of Gertrude is not meant to be sounded.

In her spiritual torment, she echoes (and confirms) Hamlet's dagger image: "O, speak to me no more. / These words like daggers enter in my ears" (3.4.95–96). The ear is especially significant in the play. Hamlet's father was poisoned in the "porches" of his ears (1.5.63), and, by metonymy for the body politic, "the whole ear of Denmark / Is by a forgèd process of my death / Rankly abused" (36–38). Hamlet's spoken daggers have been so successful in their work that the Ghost has to intervene to protect his tormented widow. Hamlet ends his soliloquy in III, ii with solemn instructions to his soul never to let his verbal assault on his mother be translated into physical action: "How in my words somever she be shent, / To give them seals never, my soul, consent!" (3.2.406–7). The proverbial-sounding couplet expresses a forbidden wish. "To be shent" is a strong expression for a rebuke verging on direct insult, a damaging reproach that might injure a person's standing or reputation. The ringing couplet makes it plain that Hamlet intends to "shend" his mother in the Closet Scene – "Let me be cruel" – even though he vows never to let his soul

consent to kill her. In this context of persistent denial, the
matricidal theme is given special emphasis. To echo Gertrude's
objection to the Player Queen, it looks as if Hamlet "doth protest
too much" (3.2.236). All of his provisoes are perilous signs.

I have been at pains to show the relation of the "Now could I
drink hot blood" soliloquy in III,ii to Hamlet's behavior in the
Closet Scene. It is not Shakespeare's usual practice to lay a scene
out so explicitly in advance, but it is entirely characteristic of his
art that, once having sounded this chorus-like overture, he doesn't
move directly to the anticipated scene between son and mother,
but rather to a displaced but analogous scene between son and
uncle-father. The crucial Prayer Scene with Hamlet and Claudius
occurs, as it were, in passing, while Hamlet with sword drawn is
passing through on his way to his mother's room. Both the Prayer
Scene and the Closet Scene are remarkable for showing us the king
and the queen in spiritual crisis. At the very moment that Hamlet
the revenger forfeits our sympathy by his relentless swagger and
cruelty, the King and the Queen are both strikingly sympathetic in
their torments of conscience. This alienation of the protagonist
from the audience's feelings in the middle of the play is a daring
structural device. In the whole movement of the play there is no
pressing reason to rehabilitate Claudius and Gertrude at the
expense of Hamlet at this point. The logic of it marks a distinct
low point for Hamlet, who will now rise steadily in our esteem.
This peripety or change in fortune is what makes for such a sharp
division between the middle and the end of the play.

In the Closet Scene, the Ghost seems to answer Gertrude's
painful appeal to her son: "O Hamlet, speak no more" (3.4.89),
"O, speak to me no more" (95), "No more" (102). "No more" is
the Ghost's cue to enter, and he manages to divert Hamlet's lurid
and oedipal preoccupation with "honeying and making love /
Over the nasty sty" (94–95). The Ghost is concerned with the
shattering physical effect Hamlet's assault has had on his mother,
since "conceit" – conception, imagination – "in weakest bodies
strongest works" (115). The way Gertrude looks at this point must
justify the Ghost's extreme concern. This is certainly the
tenderest-hearted and most domestic Ghost in all of English

literature, and its final words are a plea to its son to change his approach: "Speak to her, Hamlet" (116). Hamlet has been speaking "words like daggers" (96). He is now required to speak words of spiritual comfort and in this, of course, he fails completely.

Before Hamlet enters in the Closet Scene, we hear his anguished cries from offstage, "Mother, Mother, Mother!" (3.4.6). These "Mother" exclamations continue, with seven intervening lines of business for the King and Polonius, the tone and spirit of the end of Hamlet's soliloquy in the Prayer Scene: "And that his soul may be as damned and black / As hell, whereto it goes. My mother stays. / This physic but prolongs thy sickly days" (3.3.94–96). Since there is no pause between scenes, we hear Hamlet's "Mother, Mother, Mother!" almost immediately after the end of III,iii. If the distinction between oral and written discourse means anything at all, in oral discourse the speeches are juxtaposed both chronologically and audibly without any formal barriers between them. The oral effect depends much more significantly on echoing repetition.

Hamlet's homicidal mood, announced in the soliloquy at the end of Act III, Scene ii and demonstrated in the Prayer Scene, reaches its climax at the beginning of the Closet Scene, where there is an active possibility that Hamlet may murder his mother. Both Gertrude and Polonius seem to think so, and this gives the scene an urgency often missing from stage productions. Gertrude is genuinely frightened when Hamlet says, "Come, come, and sit you down. You shall not budge" (3.4.19). Hamlet forces his mother to sit down, and he holds her there and prevents her from moving. This is what prompts Gertrude's completely natural and highly motivated fear of matricide: "What wilt thou do? Thou wilt not murder me? Help, ho!" (22). It is as if Gertrude had been tapping into Hamlet's soliloquy at the end of Act III, Scene ii, with its talk of Nero and deliberate cruelty, a preparatory soliloquy that the audience in its omniscience knows full well. Polonius, eavesdropping from behind the arras, is convinced that Gertrude is in danger, and he echoes her cry for help: "What, ho! Help!" (24), which is presumably addressed to servants and

attendants offstage. This, of course, leads to his immediate and
unthinking murder by Hamlet: "How now? A rat? Dead for a
ducat, dead!" (25). Obviously, neither Gertrude's nor Polonius'
cries for help are heard, since no servants ever enter. Polonius is a
rat in the proverbial sense of an unwelcome intruder who cannot
be trusted. Rat also carries connotations of a deserter, spy, and
informer.

In its swaggering, colloquial style, "How now? A rat? Dead for
a ducat, dead!" seems to answer "Now might I do it pat" (3.3.73)
from the Prayer Scene. Hamlet does do it "pat" – opportunely,
aptly, just in the nick of time – and Polonius is "Dead for a ducat,
dead," as one might say for a sure bet, in which you can't help
winning the ducat wager, or when your victim is so worthless that
you will run him through for one single ducat only. This gambler's
boast of Hamlet answers, but also undercuts and trivializes, the
heroic vaunt of his soliloquy in III,ii: "Now could I drink hot blood
/ And do such business as the bitter day / Would quake to look on"
(398–400). At this point in the Closet Scene, the murder of
Polonius seems a pointless and insignificant act, mocking the
heroic pretensions of Hamlet's role as revenger.

The murder of Polonius also gives Hamlet's enemies a pretext
for moving directly against him, and Hamlet loses the bold
initiative he had seized after the triumph of the Play Scene. He is
no longer under the surveillance of the earlier part of the play, but
is now under guard, and Claudius is free to ship him off as a
prisoner to England. Even though Hamlet is "loved of the
distracted multitude" (4.3.4), the King has the excuse he needs to
get rid of him. Hamlet's constrained situation gives his long
soliloquy at the end of Act IV, Scene iv a curiously hollow ring,[5]
since he speaks as if he had complete freedom of movement and
action:

> I do not know
> Why yet I live to say, "This thing's to do,"
> Sith I have cause, and will, and strength, and means
> To do't.   (4.4.43–46)

"Thing" is a notable euphemism to avoid naming the deed itself, and the whole soliloquy soars with rhetorical declamation.

The "How all occasions do inform against me" soliloquy is the logical conclusion of the "Now could I drink hot blood" soliloquy in III,ii, and it marks the culmination – the verbal culmination at least – as well as the end of Hamlet's concerted attempt to play the revenger. He tries manfully in this soliloquy to spur his "dull revenge" (33) with arguments about dueler's honor. Like Troilus, whom he resembles in many ways, Hamlet locates honor in the eye of the beholder rather than in the intrinsic cause, so that "When honor's at the stake," the true swordsman can find matter for quarrel "in a straw" (55–56). The army of Fortinbras, marching against Poland "to gain a little patch of ground / That hath in it no profit but the name" (18–19), exhorts Hamlet to this very chivalric but distorted notion of personal honor. It is not surprising to hear him end his speech with a renewed commitment to bloody revenge: "O, from this time forth, / My thoughts be bloody, or be nothing worth!" (65–66). This is in the brave and swaggering style of Hamlet's rhetoric at the end of Act II: "Bloody, bawdy villain! / Remorseless, treacherous, lecherous, kindless villain! / O, vengeance!" (2.2.591–93). The soliloquy form allows for ringing and self-indulgent declamation that is not possible in dialogue, where the restraints are more obvious. The ironic point of the "How all occasions do inform against me" soliloquy is evident in our surprise at hearing a prisoner speak with such resolute disregard of his physical circumstances.

Perhaps Shakespeare recognized the problem here, since the whole "How all occasions do inform against me" speech has been cut from the Folio text of the play, and Hamlet doesn't appear at all in this scene, which ends at about line 8 of the Quarto 2 version from which I have been quoting.[6] Despite his strong rhetoric, Hamlet has reached an impasse in his role as revenger. His thoughts may be "bloody," but they are indeed "nothing worth" without the capacity for putting them into execution. But the revenge actions Hamlet has already taken – passing up the chance to kill Claudius at prayer to wait for a more damnable occasion, berating his mother with lurid images of sexual guilt, running Polonius through with heedless bravado – all seem particularly pointless and self-defeating, and Hamlet now awaits certain death in England. Claudius has already set in motion the final solution of the Hamlet problem.

I have been trying to argue that there is a distinct middle movement in *Hamlet*, beginning with the soliloquy at the end of Act III, Scene ii, and ending with the soliloquy at the end of Act IV, Scene iv. The purpose of this sequence is to show Hamlet as a revenger, like the "rugged Pyrrhus" (2.2.461) butchering old Priam in the Player's Speech, and also like the vaunting Laertes in the scenes that immediately follow Hamlet's departure for England. Laertes' thoughts are certainly bloody enough, as he vows to cut his enemy's throat "i' th' church" (4.7.126), and Claudius puffs him up to believe that "Revenge should have no bounds" (128). But for Hamlet there is no possible resolution in the roles of swordsman, dueler, and drinker of hot blood. That is why, when he returns from the sea voyage, the question of his revenge is set in an entirely different perspective.[7] "When our deep plots do pall" (5.2.9), the workings of Providence replace any merely personal and homicidal initiative. The sequence, therefore, from Hamlet's return to Denmark until his death, marks a final, distinctive movement in the tragedy, very different from the turbulent middle.

I know I have not presented a pleasant picture of Hamlet, ready to "drink hot blood / And do such business as the bitter day / Would quake to look on." This is Hamlet the Dane of the popular dramatic tradition rather than Hamlet the Contemplative of Romantic fancy. Yet the middle Hamlet I have sketched is also a vigorous, manly figure like other revengers in Elizabethan drama. He is trying to work out the revenger's impossible dilemma of how to take action without becoming tainted by his own violence. If Hamlet is cruel at this point, he is also forthright in telling us what he is thinking, even if it is shocking, contradictory, and perhaps also damnable. Hamlet explores and works through the revenger's role in a way not possible to Pyrrhus and Laertes, whose towering passions seem a parody of something they can never understand. Like the Players, Hamlet is unusual as a revenger in not keeping counsel and telling all (3.2.147). He ends with the ability to accept his fate with quiet resolve and New Testament lucidity: "If it be now, 'tis not to come; if it be not to come, it will be now; if it be not now, yet it will come. The readiness is all" (5.2.221–24). No other revenger in Elizabethan drama ends by being so philosophical. Hamlet is now ready to die, which is different from being ready to kill, although the two readinesses may depend on each other.

It is at this point that Christianity and Roman Stoicism intersect, and the tragic protagonist puts himself in tune with metaphysical forces. Revenge becomes a matter of general readiness rather than a matter of plotting and manipulation of circumstance. In pursuing the middle, revenge sequence of *Hamlet*, I have tried to insist on a cruder, more primitive sense of what the play is about. But the middle movement is not by any means the final word; there is still the ending, which attempts to work out the implications of the revenge theme as few other contemporary revenge plays do. It is important to Shakespeare to immerse Hamlet in the unsuccessful role of stage revenger in order to rescue him for something better at the end. We are meant to be offended with Hamlet in this middle sequence, repelled by his cruelty and crassness, and shocked by his preoccupation with sex and violence. The daring and memorable aspect of the Hamlet role is its enormous variety. Hamlet thinks, speaks, orates, and acts. By his fluidity and movement he moves us too.

7

Scene rows, broken scenes, and impacted scenes

Shakespeare's units of action are still very imperfectly understood. We lack a vocabulary to describe the structure of a Shakespearean play that will be acceptable both to literary critics and to actors, directors, and theatrical historians. We need a way of speaking about how a play is organized that would be translatable into performance. Recent thinking has done much to illuminate the scene as the basic structural unit in Shakespearean and Elizabethan drama.[1] Act-divisions have been generally discredited as a classical ornament appealing to printers and editors but inauthentic for Shakespeare and his fellow dramatists. The five-act structure is not relevant to Shakespeare except in special cases such as *Henry V*, where the prologues and choruses self-consciously divide the play as if it were a classical epic.

If the structure of a Shakespearean play depends on scenes, then we should look to the progression of scenes for the larger patterns of movement in the play. I use the term "scene row" for the organization of scenes into a single sequence or unit that functions like a single act (but may not have the same dimensions as the acts marked by Shakespeare's editors). A play need not have five scene rows to parallel the five-act structure, nor does it necessarily divide into two or three scene rows to provide for intermission breaks. "Scene rows" suggests a musical analogy with the atonal system of logically related tone rows. Perhaps music theory could be a fruitful source of a new vocabulary of structural terms for Shakespearean drama, since music presents a coherent set of analogous relationships that are governed by temporal movement. It is the pauses and breaks in the temporal movement that are significant in defining structure. They make us aware of change and discontinuity. The most obvious formula for temporal change is before and after. Shakespeare was fond of the basic two-part structure in the before-and-after sequence. Thus *Julius Caesar* is organized around events before and after the assassination of Caesar. In *Coriolanus* we have scenes before and after Coriolanus' exile from Rome, and in *The Winter's Tale* there is a sixteen-year gap at the center. Sometimes plays have two locales that are set against each other which help to define binary oppositions: Egypt and Rome in *Antony and Cleopatra*, Venice and Belmont in *The Merchant of Venice*, Venice and Cyprus in *Othello*, Athens and the wood in *A Midsummer Night's Dream*. Time and place tend to work together,[2] so that a change in place usually also signifies a change in time. Hamlet's sea voyage to England, for example, marks a radical movement in the action away from the young Hamlet who was called home from the university at Wittenberg to attend the funeral of his father. When Hamlet returns from England, we are conscious that much time has elapsed, although we are not meant to know exactly how long. Shakespeare cleverly combines a break in the temporal sequence with a mysterious voyage that represents a break in the topographical sequence.

Using the notion of discontinuities in the temporal movement to define structure, I believe we can discern four distinct dramatic units or scene rows in *Hamlet*. I realize, of course, that this scheme is tentative, since the play could be organized differently depending on the dramatic points one wishes to make, either for oneself or on Shakespeare's behalf. The first scene row is expository and covers what is generally taken to be Act I. It turns chiefly on the Ghost, including events leading up to Hamlet's encounter with the Ghost and its revelations and their aftermath. Counterpointed against the Ghost, Hamlet, Horatio, and the guards at Elsinore, we see the smooth and articulate Claudius in his court and the wily, doddering Polonius in his household. A long second sequence begins in II,i with the revelation of Polonius' politic methods of spying on his son Laertes in Paris and Hamlet at home. The mad Hamlet is clearly in danger – he may be the man who knows too much – and the presence of Rosencrantz and Guildenstern intensifies the conflict. The scenes with the Players and the *Mousetrap* play that catches the conscience of the King seem to give Hamlet the initiative, which culminates with the King's rising to break up the play and beat a hasty retreat.

Hamlet's imminent visit with his mother marks the aftermath of his triumph in the Play Scene and the beginning of a third sequence, which opens with Hamlet's soliloquy at the end of III,ii. Throughout this third scene row (or middle of the play) Hamlet is trying out the role of revenger, a point abundantly evident in the Prayer Scene with Claudius and the Closet Scene with Gertrude, which culminates in the murder of Polonius and Hamlet's departure on the sea voyage that is supposed to lead to his sudden death in England. The break between the third and the fourth scene rows is the most strongly marked division in the play. With Hamlet safely out of the way, the fourth scene row begins in Act IV, Scene v with the madness of Ophelia, but Laertes' rebellion immediately alerts us to a counter-movement against Claudius. The King brilliantly diverts the foolish Laertes to his own purposes at the same time as we become aware of Hamlet's escape from the pirates and return to Elsinore. Everything moves inevitably toward the fencing match, during which Gertrude, Hamlet, Laertes, and Claudius are killed. In the dénouement Fortinbras becomes the new ruler of Denmark; he has Hamlet's "dying voice" (5.2.357).

One could, of course, arrange the scenes differently within this four-part structure. The Polonius scene in II,i, for example, could serve as an ironic afterpiece to the Ghost sequence. But it is difficult to conceive more or less than four basic units. This doesn't work well for a five-act play, nor does it fit into a two-part sequence of before and after or two locales. Directors can put the intermission (or intermissions) where they would conveniently suit the needs of the actors, the audience, and the concessionaires, but a break is most logical at the end of the second sequence after the Play Scene, where most productions in fact have it. If a second intermission is needed, it should come at the point where Hamlet is shipped off to England at the end of Act IV, Scene iv. We would like to believe that *Hamlet* was presented without any breaks at all in Shakespeare's time – "the two hours' traffic of our stage" (Prologue to *Romeo and Juliet*) – but we can't be sure. Our present text of *Hamlet* is usually a conflation of Quarto 2 and Folio (with some touches preserved from Quarto 1) – a text which never existed of course. By themselves the Quarto 2 or the Folio versions are shorter than the conflated version, and Quarto 1 is very short indeed.

The scene rows of *Hamlet* are composed of at least two different kinds of units: broken scenes and impacted scenes. A broken scene is essentially a single scene that is broken into two or more parts separated from each other by an impacted scene or scenes. In other words, by breaking a continuous action into several scenes Shakespeare can omit parts of the full narrative. The impacted scene or scenes that come in the midst of the broken scene provide a temporal bridge which would account for the passage of time. The impacted scene covers a narrative jump. Once the straight narrative flow (or "story line") of a scene is interrupted, the dramatist can then pick it up again at a point much later in time. The intervening events are presumed to take place during the bridge scene or impacted scene wedged between the two parts of the broken scene.

Act IV, Scene v and Act IV, Scene vii work well together in this progressive sense. Laertes' rebellion in IV,v is completely successful, and it looks as if Claudius will be made a prisoner and Laertes will seize the throne of Denmark. But Claudius wheedles and bullies his way into Laertes' confidence; he challenges him and placates him at the same time. By the end of IV,v, the King has persuaded Laertes and whatever impartial judges he may choose to "hear and judge 'twixt you and me" (4.5.203). We never hear anything further about these "wisest friends" (202), but Laertes' curiosity has been piqued and we are certain that the King can now do as he pleases with him. In response to Laertes' irritated inquiry into his father's hugger-mugger funeral that cries "to be heard, as 'twere from heaven to earth, / That I must call't in question" (214–15), Claudius says composedly, "So you shall" (215). He is teasing the angry youth along.

The next scene (IV,vi) does not continue IV,v. We shift

abruptly to a brief impacted scene of Horatio and the Pirates[3] and news of Hamlet's escape from certain death in England. Hamlet's letter in IV,vi is unusually vigorous, energetic, and satirical; it is a preparation for his breezy escape narrative to Horatio at the beginning of V,ii. We are already seeing a new Hamlet more capable of working out his own destiny than when shipped to England under guard at the end of IV,iv. Hamlet's tone in IV,vi catches something of the swagger of the Pirate Sailors who deliver the letter. The Sailor's "God bless you, sir" to Horatio, is answered by Horatio's "Let Him bless thee too," with the implication that a pirate sailor would stand in need of God's blessing. The Sailor answers him with a certain fierce impudence: " 'A shall, sir, an't please Him" (4.6.7–9), rather than if it pleases Horatio. The King will soon learn that Hamlet is not so easily destroyed, and Hamlet, Horatio, and the Pirate Sailors together appear formidable antagonists for Claudius and Laertes.

When the Laertes-Claudius scene (IV,v) is resumed in IV,vii, the King has already fully convinced Laertes of his innocence in Polonius' death. In the imagined offstage action, a great deal has happened between the end of IV,v – "And where th' offense is, let the great ax fall" (216) – and the beginning of IV,vii – "Now must your conscience my acquittance seal, / And you must put me in your heart for friend" (1–2). The persuasion of Laertes is finished – more properly, it has never occurred on stage at all – and the King now awaits, with great self-satisfaction, the crowning news of Hamlet's death in England. "You shortly shall hear more" (4.7.33), says Claudius with heavy implication. That news will indeed seal him in Laertes' heart "for friend."

To Claudius' ill-concealed astonishment, a messenger enters with letters from the recently escaped Hamlet. This is indeed a *coup de théâtre* and we are back in the exciting narrative mode of IV,vi. Although he is "set naked" (4.7.43–44) in Claudius' kingdom, Hamlet's letter is menacingly satirical and directly challenges the King's complacency with Laertes. There is a good deal of mystification connected with this letter. The anonymous messenger claims that the letter was brought by sailors, whom he did not see, and given to him by Claudio who "received them [the letters] / Of him that brought them" (4.7.40–41). Incidentally, the name Claudio is dangerously close to that of the King, who is never actually called Claudius in the play. IV,vi and IV,vii together juxtapose action and counter-action, Laertes and Claudius vs. the newly escaped Hamlet. The news of his escape serves as a counter-weight to the reconciliation of Laertes and Claudius. Hamlet is ready for them as they are making ready for him.

Now unfolds the triple plot against Hamlet that must be devised on the spur of the moment. Claudius knows how to provoke Laertes with ingeniously disarming questions:

> Laertes, was your father dear to you?
> Or are you like the painting of a sorrow
> A face without a heart? (4.7.107–9)

> what would you undertake
> To show yourself in deed your father's son
> More than in words? (4.7.124–26)

The innocent and manipulable Laertes is goaded to utter what can only be understood as a strange mixture of blasphemy, heroic vaunting, and old-fashioned rant: "To cut his throat i' th' church" (126). Even Claudius is taken aback by this unseemly answer to what he intended as a rhetorical question; he knows that his pep talk is definitely over.

The news of Ophelia's death gives Claudius another unquiet moment after Laertes has exited at the end of the scene:

> Let's follow, Gertrude.
> How much I had to do to calm his rage!
> Now fear I this will give it start again;
> Therefore let's follow. (4.7.191–94)

It is typical of Claudius to want to control everything and not let anything slip through his fingers.

By breaking the scene between Claudius and Laertes into IV,v and IV,vii, Shakespeare accomplishes several different things. The potentially tedious persuasion of Laertes can be left out. This is an important narrative economy at a moment when the action is moving swiftly to the catastrophe. Hamlet's letter and the interpolated and impacted scene with the Pirate Sailors offer an ironic commentary on the King's smug assurance that Hamlet has been assassinated in England. Claudius is made to worry, so that he pushes Laertes far beyond anything we might have expected. Laertes unwittingly becomes another bloody Pyrrhus. IV,vi also sets in motion a counter-action against Claudius and Laertes. Time is running out, and we are moving relentlessly toward the fencing match and the general slaughter that end the play.

The first scene row in *Hamlet*, focusing on the Ghost, also makes important use of broken scenes and impacted scenes. Hamlet is not permitted to encounter the Ghost in the first scene. Through the anxieties of Barnardo, Francisco, Marcellus, and Horatio, we build toward later encounters with the Ghost when Hamlet will be present. At the end of the scene, Horatio resolves to "impart what we have seen tonight / Unto young Hamlet, for upon my life / This spirit, dumb to us, will speak to him" (1.1.169–71). In Scene ii Horatio tells Hamlet about the Ghost (189ff.), but this scene is essentially an impacted one, since the Ghost action is suspended and we have a colorful public display of Claudius beginning his reign. Scene iii takes us further afield to the Polonius household, where both Laertes and Polonius advise Ophelia to break off her love affair with Hamlet. We don't return to the Ghost until Scenes iv and v, which are really a single continuous scene. Although the stage is cleared at 1.4.91, Hamlet and the Ghost re-enter immediately at what editors mark as Scene v.

What is impacted between the two (or three) parts of the broken Ghost scene? The slick Claudius of Act I, Scene ii is seen to be a powerful antagonist. He dispatches the business of state with alarming directness. The danger that young Fortinbras represents to the state of Denmark is contemptuously minimized: "So much for him. / Now for ourself" (1.2.25–26). This is in the style of the resolute Claudius of Act IV, Scene vii, jollifying Laertes:

> You must not think
> That we are made of stuff so flat and dull
> That we can let our beard be shook with danger,
> And think it pastime. (4.7.30–33)

We know nothing definite about the King, but there is something disquieting about the gap between his unctuous public language and his quiet determination to rule.

In the second scene the reality of the Ghost is revived by Horatio's awesome narration to Hamlet of what happened in the first scene. This account replays the original scene for Hamlet, who, like Horatio, is harrowed "with fear and wonder" (1.1.44). In the brief soliloquy that ends this scene, Hamlet's fears match those of Horatio and the soldiers: "All is not well. / I doubt some foul play" (1.2.255–56). There is an almost automatic assumption of "Foul deeds," which "will rise, / Though all the earth o'erwhelm them, to men's eyes" (1.2.257–58). By breaking the Ghost scene into several discontinuous parts, the play builds suspense and anticipation.

The scene that follows (I,iii) with Laertes, Ophelia, and Polonius feels like a diversion. We are in the comforting atmosphere of the Polonius household with plenty of parental advice both to son and daughter: "these few precepts in thy memory / Look thou character" (58–59). But we already know from the previous scene that Polonius, as chief counselor of state, has some insidious and unexplained relation to the King, who is excessively grateful to him for helping him to the throne. Young Laertes, a potential ally of Hamlet, is being eagerly sent off to Paris, and Ophelia is brutally sequestered from Hamlet, who loves her. Act I, Scene iii is disturbing because underneath its comfortable and cozy domesticity lie threats and cajolery.

The Ghost scenes represent the night world of *Hamlet* and stand at an opposite pole from the animated and active daytime scenes at court and in Polonius' household. In Scene iv we return suddenly to the cold, windy, midnight scene on the battlements of Elsinore. There is an air of mystery about revelations from beyond the grave. We feel strongly that "Something is rotten in the state of Denmark" (1.4.90), but we are also sure that we will not receive clarification from Claudius' court or Polonius' household. Those are the pasteboard masks that we need to pierce, the false show, the deceptive appearance. The Ghost's narration is astounding but not unanticipated. We are, in fact, relieved that at last we have something to go on, that we are no longer in the dark. Should we believe the Ghost? At this moment we have no other choice, since there is no counter-explanation that we may seize on. Hamlet is now ready to sweep to his revenge, but we know from I,ii and I,iii that there are powerful obstacles in his path.

Act I, Scene iv deliberately recapitulates phrases and tones from the Ghost scene at the beginning of the play: "The air bites shrewdly; it is very cold. / It is a nipping and an eager air" (1.4.1–2) – "eager" in the sense of pungent, acrid, sharp, like vinegar. The first scene is being replayed on another night and with Hamlet as principal actor. In typical broken-scene fashion, it uses the previous impacted scenes (I,ii and I,iii) as context. The second Ghost scenes (I,iv and I,v) rely on narrative economy, and they need fewer explanations. We begin, logically, almost at the end of the Ghost scene proper when Hamlet and the Ghost will speak freely and fully and face to face. All ambiguities are about to be cleared up.

The broken Ghost scenes in *Hamlet* allow us to move quickly to the essential exposition on which the entire play turns. Our doubts and quandaries are at least partially resolved. By breaking the Ghost action into two (or three) parts, the later parts can absorb the values of the impacted scenes that occur in between. We know that Hamlet is not an isolated figure, that he has formidable opponents, and that his revenger's ardor cannot last. In sum, the breaking of what might have been one single scene gives scope to analogy, so that we may feel the full force of dramatic conflict. Action and counter-action work powerfully against each other, and the Ghost is the catalyst to purge the rottenness in the state of Denmark.

The third scene row of Hamlet as revenger also develops a broken scene as Hamlet is on his way to his mother's closet (III,iv). In Hamlet's soliloquy at the end of Act III, Scene ii, he prepares himself for the encounter: "Soft, now to my mother" (400). The substance of the soliloquy is that Hamlet is steeling himself against matricide. We know his preoccupations unusually well at this point, but the soliloquy has no immediate aftermath, and we shift immediately to an impacted scene of the King and Rosencrantz and Guildenstern (III,iii). Polonius enters on his fateful errand to hide himself behind the arras in Gertrude's closet so that he may overhear the mother's interview with her son.

Finally, at line 36, Claudius is alone, and he moves into his powerful soliloquy acknowledging his guilt and hoping to pray for forgiveness. This soliloquy is crucial for understanding the Closet Scene, since Gertrude too is repentant and we need our own image of Claudius to set against those of Gertrude, Hamlet, and the Ghost. Into this scene of Claudius attempting to pray comes Prince Hamlet on his way to his mother's closet with his sword drawn – he doesn't sheathe it until line 88 ("Up sword"). In this sequence, time seems to be exaggeratedly slowed down as Hamlet proceeds from his soliloquy at the end of III,ii to his mother's closet. On this prolonged journey, he comes upon his uncle praying and debates whether this is a good moment to kill him and be revenged. It isn't. It's hard to imagine the Closet Scene without the Prayer Scene as its context. The Closet Scene is not exactly broken into separate parts, but the elaborate preparation of Hamlet in the soliloquy at the end of III,ii is deliberately suspended while we watch the Prayer Scene. Hamlet is artfully brought through Claudius' closet to bring the two scenes into juxtaposition.

Ophelia's mad scene in Act IV, Scene v is broken so that she can be made to appear twice, once to the Queen and King and Horatio, and then to the King and Queen and Laertes. In the midst of this broken scene, we have Laertes' rebellion. Essentially, Ophelia has two mad scenes instead of one. Her second appearance has as its context her first appearance and also Laertes' rebellion. In her second appearance, her brother dominates the scene, and his reaction to his mad sister underscores the political action: "Hadst thou thy wits, and didst persuade revenge, / It could not move thus" (4.5.168–69). The mad Ophelia reinforces the need to revenge their murdered father, and Claudius is put on his mettle to offer attractive conditions he has no intention of fulfilling. If Laertes' "wisest friends" "find us touched, we will our kingdom give, / Our crown, our life, and all that we call ours, / To you in satisfaction" (4.5.204–6). It is typical of Claudius to take what seem to others as dangerous risks, but in which the King himself risks nothing. The Ophelia action is deliberately broken into significant and carefully spaced segments. At the end of IV,vii, the Queen reports Ophelia's drowning in a lyrically flamboyant speech, and in V,i Ophelia is buried with conspicuous lack of ceremony. In the dramatic economy there is an obvious need to fragment what happens to Ophelia into separate scenes or pieces of scenes. Since she is a minor character, our interest tends to focus on how she relates to other more important characters such as Hamlet, Laertes, and Claudius. Her mad scene in IV,v is the only one she is permitted to dominate.

The way the scene rows in *Hamlet* are devised suggests that Shakespeare used a method of scenic construction and juxtaposition similar to montage in the movies. The most obvious point about the relation of the scenes is that they emphasize narrative and chronological discontinuity. Shakespeare was fond of breaking what seems to be a single piece of action into several parts that occur in different contexts and which generally leave out the middle of the narrative. The use of impacted scenes wedged into the spaces between the broken scenes helps to create a sense of radical contrast. Nothing is allowed to move forward in a straight line. A scene row is built up of representative and typical pieces, some related directly and others related only by analogy. There is the sense of a mosaic rather than a continuous flow. In the movies we keep cutting from one action to another, with seemingly unrelated atmospheric and poetic details in between. Yet everything coheres through our desire to establish order out of miscellaneous fragments. We impose the connections that are missing in the text so that it is unnecessary to fill out the jumps and cuts in the narrative. We remember how Hamlet wittily objects to the excessive fullness of the *Mousetrap* play: "The players cannot keep counsel; they'll tell all" (3.2.146–47). Shakespeare is obviously committed to not telling all.

PART III

CONVENTIONS OF STAGING, IMAGERY, AND GENRE

8

The stage situation of asides, soliloquies, and offstage speech

The frozen, stream-of-consciousness soliloquies and asides in Eugene O'Neill's *Strange Interlude* (1928), which always seemed such a stumbling block to performance, were beautifully integrated into the play in Keith Hack's recent revival in London (1984) and New York (1985). The principal characters, especially those played by Edward Petherbridge and Glenda Jackson, made no obvious distinction between public speech and private reflection. The soliloquies and asides were spoken in the same voice as ordinary dialogue and made continuous with it, so that there was no way for the characters to hide, as O'Neill said, "behind the sounds called words." Keith Hack's production went against O'Neill's symbolic division between the inner and outer play, public and private speech, yet he managed to make the Elizabethan conventions believable and fluid, whereas in O'Neill's conception they are heavy, static, rhetorical, and moralistic.[1]

This continuity between the conventional speech of soliloquy and aside and ordinary dialogue throws retrospective light on Shakespearean and Elizabethan practice. In order to be effective dramatically, soliloquy and aside cannot be either interruptive or segregated from the rest of the play. There can be no special soliloquy and aside voice which highlights these conventional utterances, nor do most soliloquies and asides provide a window into the souls of the characters. Critics have misguidedly used the soliloquies and asides of *Hamlet* to psychologize the play and to transform it from an exciting revenge action into a novel of inner revelation. There is a tendency to overstate the function of soliloquies and asides as if they were the core of the real, private play of consciousness while the external, public play swirled meaninglessly around us. Francis Berry has reminded us in *The Shakespeare Inset*[2] how much non-dialogue there is in a typical play by Shakespeare, so that soliloquy and aside are not the only devices interrupting the dialogic flow. Shakespearean drama is based upon narrative and other discontinuities, and it is structured as a montage of significant pieces of action that serve as a synecdoche for an action which may be fully imagined but is never presented in its entirety. We have already taken up, in Chapter 7, the use of broken scenes and impacted scenes to secure this effect.

I

One example of the "privatization" of *Hamlet*, or the attempt to convert the public play into a psychological, inner drama of conscience, is the excessive number of asides claimed for the action. Most modern editions print Hamlet's first words, "A little more than kin, and less than kind!" (1.2.65), as an aside, following Theobald's second edition of 1740. But this is clearly intended as bitterly ironic, punning, public speech. The isolated Hamlet, still in mourning, is attacking the gaudy cheerfulness of Claudius' court. If his words were an aside, the satirical outrage would be muted.

In the Play Scene, Hamlet's sardonic comment "That's wormwood" (3.2.187) to the Player Queen's protestation, "In second husband let me be accurst! / None wed the second but who killed the first" (185–96), is hardly an aside, despite all the editors who have followed Capell (1768). Like "A little more than kin, and less than kind," "That's wormwood" is an interruptive, public comment on the play like those of the onstage audiences to "Pyramus and Thisby" in *A Midsummer Night's Dream* and the play of the Nine Worthies in *Love's Labor's Lost*. Hamlet plays the all-knowing wiseguy in this scene. His antic disposition, which no one fully believes in any longer, gives him license to make wisecracks and to act the part of what we would call a kibitzer. "That's wormwood" is spoken not to relieve the prince's private tensions but to taunt the audience and to express publicly his disdain for the tedious old *Mousetrap* play.

The most important asides in *Hamlet* are those that express guilty conscience: the King's, the Queen's, and Laertes'. These "solo" asides (in the terminology of Bernard Beckerman[3]) all function like brief soliloquies, but their purpose is so compact and so deliberate that they seem excessively expository. In other words, they serve the needs of the play at the expense of the immediate context of the character speaking and the development of the dramatic action. The most blatant in this regard is the aside of Claudius just before Hamlet's "To be, or not to be" soliloquy. Both Claudius and Polonius will be lawful espials for Hamlet's soliloquy, and the King's aside answers Polonius' crass remarks to Ophelia as she is set up as a decoy for Hamlet:

> Read on this book,
> That show of such an exercise may color
> Your loneliness. We are oft to blame in this,
> 'Tis too much proved, that with devotion's visage
> And pious action we do sugar o'er
> The devil himself.   (3.1.44–49)

Ophelia and her prayer book echo the emblematic representation of Richard, Duke of Gloucester, according to Buckingham's instructions: "And look you get a prayer book in your hand / And stand between two churchmen" (*Richard III* 3.7.46–47). It is the essence of hypocrisy.

The King's aside continues the moral platitudes and pat style of Polonius' speech:

> O, 'tis too true.
> How smart a lash that speech doth give my conscience!
> The harlot's cheek, beautied with plast'ring art,
> Is not more ugly to the thing that helps it
> Than is my deed to my most painted word.
> O heavy burden!   (3.1.49–54)

This anticipates Claudius' soliloquy in the Prayer Scene ("O, my offense is rank" 3.3.36ff.), and it is the first confirmation of his guilt for the audience. It corroborates the Ghost's narration in

Act I, Scene v. We can understand why this aside would be important, structurally, as a context for Hamlet's "To be, or not to be" soliloquy, yet the aside itself is painfully obvious. It is inserted into the play in a schematic form that would be more appropriate for Polonius than for the King. It is not until the Prayer Scene (III,iii) that we come to understand the King's confessional but not fully repentant frame of mind.

The King's aside does its expository work at the expense of dramatic vividness and full characterization. The Queen's couplet aside in IV,v is similarly frigid and didactic:

> To my sick soul (as sin's true nature is)
> Each toy seems prologue to some great amiss;
> So full of artless jealousy is guilt
> It spills itself in fearing to be spilt.
>
> (4.5.17–20)

The Queen, who had at first refused to speak with the mad Ophelia, is finally persuaded by Horatio and a nameless Gentleman to "Let her come in" (4.5.16). Gertrude's expression of guilt recalls the Closet Scene (III,iv), but the brevity and epigrammatic form of the couplets tend to work against the characterization of Gertrude, who sounds more like the Player Queen of *The Mousetrap* than the grieving and heartsick mother and recent widow of the Closet Scene. The jingle of "So full of artless jealousy is guilt / It spills itself in fearing to be spilt" echoes the formulaic sentiments of the Player Queen: "Both here and hence pursue me lasting strife, / If, once a widow, ever I be wife!" (3.2.228–29). The aside is unworthy of Gertrude at this point; we had expected something more acute and more revealing.

It is curious that the most important asides in *Hamlet* are so thoroughly didactic, as if they served a moral function different from dialogue. In the final scene of the play, the strenuous effort to rehabilitate Laertes and to reconcile him with Hamlet is partly accomplished by Laertes' aside: "And yet it is almost against my conscience" (5.2.297). In the immediate context, the Queen has already drunk from the poisoned chalice prepared for Hamlet, and the King registers his stoic shock in a factual aside: "It is the poisoned cup; it is too late" (293). Laertes is now determined to score in the fencing match by fair means or foul: "My lord, I'll hit him now," but the King is not convinced: "I do not think't" (296). It is at this point, before the foul play that will kill Hamlet is unleashed, that Laertes expresses in an aside his moral regret: "And yet it is almost against my conscience."

How typical of Laertes is the sentimental, moral equivocation in "*almost* against my conscience," as if there were some way to excuse or palliate his dirty deed. This reservation recalls Laertes' cagey answer to Hamlet's open-hearted desire for forgiveness. Laertes stands "aloof" in his "terms of honor" until "some elder masters of known honor" will provide a "precedent of peace" to keep his "name ungored" (5.2.247–51). The legalism of these bogus formulas is still touched on in "almost." Laertes' aside is not fully frank and candid, and it seems peculiarly unrelated to the dramatic context. It is, in essence, a moral declaration rather than a thought or feeling that impinges on the immediate action. The asides of Laertes, Gertrude, and Claudius may be grouped together by their artificiality, their deliberateness, and their attempt to make large moral points that are not necessarily those of the dramatic context.

The more conventional asides of *Hamlet* tend to be brief comments that establish a point for the audience, usually an expository point about "some necessary question of the play" (3.2.44–45). We have already noticed the King's aside: "It is the poisoned cup; it is too late" (5.2.293), by which we know that Claudius will tough it out to the end and make no unnecessary compassionate gestures. This example makes a clear distinction between public and private discourse; the King cannot afford to make any public declarations or to intervene to save the Queen. The aside is a convenient acknowledgment of "purposes mistook / Fall'n on th' inventors' heads" (5.2.385–86).

Polonius has a series of explanatory asides in the Fishmonger Scene with Hamlet by which he asserts both his platitudinous wisdom and his patronizing superiority to the "mad" Hamlet. One key point is that Polonius is impervious to wordplay. In his asides he appeals to the lowest common denominator of the audience to

help him make out what Hamlet might be saying. To Hamlet's
"Conception is a blessing, but as your daughter may conceive,
friend, look to't" (2.2.185–87), Polonius can only reply by missing
the point of the pun:

> How say you by that? Still harping on my daughter. Yet he
> knew me not at first. 'A said I was a fishmonger. 'A is far gone,
> far gone. And truly in my youth I suffered much extremity for
> love, very near this. I'll speak to him again.   (2.2.188–92)

Notice how self-consciously markers are put in to separate the
aside from the dialogue that follows. Polonius makes a point of
telling us: "I'll speak to him again." It is as if the old counselor in
his asides needs to be in cahoots with the audience to whom the
asides are directed. He speaks only with their implied permission
and complicity because he assumes that they too are having trouble
understanding Hamlet's wild and whirling words.

As the dialogue proceeds, however, Polonius becomes more and
more convinced of the truth of his next aside: "Though this be
madness, yet there is method in't" (2.2.207–8). In other words,
Hamlet is more calculating than he previously appeared to be, less
spontaneous and more artful – in fact, more like Polonius himself.
This is the conclusion of Polonius' final aside in this sequence:

> How pregnant sometimes his replies are! A happiness that often
> madness hits on, which reason and sanity could not so
> prosperously be delivered of. I will leave him and suddenly
> contrive the means of meeting between him and my daughter.
>   (2.2.210–15)

"Pregnant" means "loaded, charged," in the sense that Polonius is
aware of satirical connotations he cannot explicitly identify, but
the *double entendre* fits very nicely with the sexual fears of father and
son that Ophelia will open her "chaste treasure" to Hamlet's
"unmastered importunity" (1.3.31–32). In a similar exchange after
the *Mousetrap* play, Hamlet twits Polonius with the cloud shapes –
camel, weasel, whale – yet it is Hamlet himself who feels put upon
and toyed with, as he exclaims in an irritable aside: "They fool me
to the top of my bent" (3.2.392). Presumably he means that

Polonius and other officious attendants of the King force him to play the uncongenial role of fool in order to protect himself.

Hamlet's asides with Rosencrantz and Guildenstern illustrate the mingling of what Beckerman calls solo and conversational asides, which are here analogous in function. Hamlet begins his dialogue with Rosencrantz and Guildenstern in a friendly enough fashion, but his confidence is gradually eroded as his old friends begin to probe like spies. Hamlet wants to determine if they "were sent for or no" (2.2.296). At this point Rosencrantz turns to Guildenstern for a classic conversational aside: "What say you?" (297). By the workings of dramatic convention, Hamlet cannot overhear this question, but he can observe the gesture that accompanies it: "Nay then, I have an eye of you" (298). We are just on the edge of the aside convention here, and Hamlet's remark to the audience is not much different in function from Rosencrantz's question to Guildenstern. Both assume that the audience is the ultimate repository and arbiter of the asides spoken on stage.

Another conversational aside occurs in the scene between Osric and Hamlet and Horatio. Hamlet objects to Osric's affected word "carriages" for "hangers," so that Horatio's aside to Hamlet underscores the foppish diction: "I knew you must be edified by the margent ere you had done" (5.2.156–57). The margin ("margent") of a printed text explains difficult words and allusions. Osric, of course, cannot overhear the insulting *badinage* contained in the aside.

The conversational asides in *Hamlet* tend to occur in longer sequences in which one group of characters is set against another. These extended asides are sometimes labeled "apart," since the stage is divided into speakers and commentators. There are two long examples in Act V, Scene i, where Hamlet and Horatio observe the gravediggers, then join them in dialogue, then stand apart to comment on the funeral of Ophelia until Hamlet can no longer bear to listen to the public discourse without breaking in. The asides serve to insulate Hamlet and Horatio from the onstage action, so that they can function as observers before they become participants. Perhaps the aside convention also suggests a new role for Hamlet as a contemplative looker-on. These asides in V,i are remarkably explicit, especially in their indications of when Hamlet and Horatio move out of the apart position and join the general conversation.

Hamlet and Horatio enter "*afar off*" (5.1.56 s.d.) at the end of the Clown-gravedigger's conversation with his assistant, who exits at line 61. The gravedigger then sings various ballads and throws up skulls, while Hamlet and Horatio comment on the "easiness" (69) of his employment. The gravedigger is an acknowledged straightman for Hamlet's meditations on mortality. Hamlet then comes forward with a specific comment to cover his action: "I will speak to this fellow" (119). This is followed by a wit combat with the Clown-gravedigger like that of the earlier match between the gravedigger and his assistant.

When the King, the Queen, Laertes, and others enter with Ophelia's coffin, Hamlet and Horatio again assume the apart position at one side of the stage: "Couch we awhile, and mark" (224). Hamlet instructs Horatio about the participants in the scene: "That is Laertes, / A very noble youth. Mark" (225–26). "Mark" indicates the act of attention demanded from observers apart. It takes Hamlet a remarkably long time to figure out that this is a funeral procession for the dead Ophelia, but once he does so he can no longer remain apart. There is an element of real danger for the newly returned Hamlet to discover himself, but he cannot tolerate Laertes' inflated rhetoric: "What is he whose grief / Bears such an emphasis . . . . This is I, / Hamlet the Dane" (256–57, 259–60). They are soon grappling in Ophelia's grave, if we follow the stage direction of Quarto 1: "*Hamlet leapes in after Laertes.*" This grotesque stage business is confirmed in an elegy on the death of Richard Burbage on March 13, 1618:

> Oft haue I seene him, leap into the Graue
> Suiting the person, which he seem'd to haue
> Of a sadd louer, with soe true an Eye
> That theer I would haue sworne, he meant to dye. . .[4]

Horatio speaks only one wise line in this part of the scene: "Good my lord, be quiet" (267).

Once they have revealed themselves, Hamlet and Horatio can

no longer return to the apart position, and one wonders how the scene was staged to render them invisible to the Clown-gravedigger and his assistant and, later, to the funeral party. There must have been well understood conventions about the privileged status of the observer apart so that his actions and movements would not seem awkward or intrusive. It adds a significant dimension to have an onstage commentator to mediate between the play and the audience. The observer apart in his asides suggests how we should react to what we see before us.

II

The stage situation of the asides in *Hamlet* is generally more interesting than that of the soliloquies, although there is a strong continuity between the two types of discourse. Some of the longer asides, such as those of the King ("How smart a lash" 3.1.49–54) and the Queen ("To my sick soul" 4.5.17–20) are analogous to soliloquies in which characters make important revelations. The distinction is based on whether the speaker is alone on stage, although in some soliloquies the speaker may think he is alone but actually isn't. For all practical purposes, soliloquy and aside have the same dramatic function in relation to the audience. We are speaking, of course, of solo asides; conversational asides work differently. It is remarkable how many soliloquies end with couplets, especially scene-ending couplets, which would tend to emphasize the speech's rhetorical purpose. There are also many markers to set off the soliloquy from ordinary dialogue, like Hamlet's "Now I am alone" (2.2.559) which prefaces the "O, what a rogue and peasant slave am I" soliloquy. Throughout the play we are made distinctly aware of the soliloquy situation, which is often self-consciously prepared.

In Hamlet's first soliloquy, "O that this too too sullied flesh would melt" (1.2.129), he is suddenly alone after a "Flourish" during which Claudius and his entire court exit. There is an enormous contrast between the King's boastful account of his "rouse" – the drinking of healths accompanied by the firing of cannon, which "the heaven shall bruit again, / Respeaking earthly thunder" (127–28) – and Hamlet's mournful contemplation of non-being. When Hamlet sees Horatio, Marcellus, and Barnardo entering, he knows that his soliloquy is over and that he must once more return to public dialogue: "But break my heart, for I must hold my tongue" (159). The soliloquy is identified as a freer and more expressive medium. Hamlet must hold his tongue not in the sense that he must be mute, but only that he must return to social discourse in which he cannot speak his heart.

Hamlet has another brief soliloquy at the end of this scene that acknowledges the appearance of the Ghost. This ends with a ringing couplet of high resolution:

> Till then sit still, my soul. Foul deeds will rise,
> Though all the earth o'erwhelm them, to men's eyes.
>   (1.2.257–58)

This four-line soliloquy is not meditative in any way but expresses with great vigor Hamlet's anticipation of the Ghost's report of "Foul deeds," which echoes the proverbial formula: "murder will out."

"O, what a rogue and peasant slave am I" (2.2.560) is Hamlet's longest soliloquy (58 lines) and it goes through at least three distinct movements: his reaction to the Player's weeping for Hecuba, his revulsion at his own inflated rhetoric – "Why, what an ass am I! This is most brave" (594) – and his plan to "catch the conscience of the King" (617) with a play. According to popular psychology confirmed by various miraculous examples from real life, "guilty creatures sitting at a play" could be trapped to confess "by the very cunning of the scene" (601–2). The soliloquy has a strong feeling of sequence and narrative movement. It is the greatest showpiece of all the soliloquies in the play, and it too ends with a memorable, ringing couplet:

> The play's the thing
> Wherein I'll catch the conscience of the King.
>   (2.2.616–17)

Hamlet is riding high in this soliloquy. There is no sense in its vigorous exhortation that he is in any way inadequate for revenge.

Hamlet's "To be, or not to be" (3.1.56) soliloquy is unusual in its stage situation because Hamlet is not alone on stage. We are aware of the fact that Polonius and the King, lawful espials, "withdraw" at line 55 and remain behind the arras. When they come on stage again at the end of the scene (line 164), it is quite clear that they know all. As Polonius says to his daughter, "You need not tell us what Lord Hamlet said; / We heard it all" (182–83). Nothing explicit is said about Hamlet's soliloquy and there is no verbal indication that they have overheard it, yet we are still conscious of the fact that they are concealed behind the arras. The King and Polonius are clearly observers of the Nunnery Scene with Ophelia that follows immediately after the soliloquy.

We tend to forget that Ophelia, too, is on stage for the entire time of Hamlet's soliloquy, making it one of the most crowded soliloquies in all of Shakespeare. Ophelia has been staged by her clever father with a prayer book, to "color," or give a pretext for, her "loneliness" (45–46) or aloneness waiting on stage to encounter Hamlet. What is she doing during the time of his soliloquy? Presumably she is so preoccupied with her devotions that she doesn't notice the very person she is looking for, and Hamlet is so eager to unburden himself that he isn't aware of his old girlfriend stuck away in one corner of the stage. The very attempt to give naturalistic explanations for highly conventional stage situations reveals the absurdity of setting two kinds of theatrical reasoning against each other.

Ophelia is very much there, and we should certainly not be allowed to forget that Claudius and Polonius are behind the arras – perhaps the arras is made to stir lightly from time to time to remind us – while Hamlet delivers what he earnestly believes to be (confirmed by the judgment of posterity) his most important soliloquy in the play. At the end of the speech, he suddenly notices Ophelia: "Soft you now, / The fair Ophelia!" (88–89). "Soft" is an all-purpose Elizabethan exclamation to indicate mild surprise, and it means something like "what have we here?" Anticipating the Prayer Scene with Claudius (III,iii), Hamlet also believes that Ophelia is really praying, making "orisons" (89), or formal devotions, in which Hamlet hopes that all of his sins will be "remembered" (90). Despite the ingenious theories of John Dover Wilson,[5] Hamlet seems to have no inkling that Ophelia's orisons have been staged and that her father and Claudius are just behind the arras as observers. The staging ironies of this scene are strictly dramatic ironies for the benefit of the audience.

It is also worth noting that Hamlet's "To be, or not to be" soliloquy is set back to back with Claudius' confessional aside, "O, 'tis too true. / How smart a lash that speech doth give my conscience!" (3.1.49–50). It seems important for Shakespeare to juxtapose these two expressions of conscience. The distinction between aside and soliloquy here is more one of length and formal staging than of content. The King's aside is the immediate context for Hamlet's matching soliloquy, as if one needed the other to complete its meaning.

Ophelia's soliloquy after Hamlet's violent diatribe against women in the Nunnery Scene is elegiac in tone. It makes no answer at all to Hamlet's demands – "To a nunnery, go, and quickly too" (3.1.141–42) – but mourns the loss of Hamlet as he used to be, "Th' expectancy and rose of the fair state, / The glass of fashion, and the mold of form, / Th' observed of all observers" (155–57). It is a tragic lamentation for the disappearance of all that was once so beautiful, and Ophelia herself, like Desdemona in the Willow Scene, can only grieve for all that has happened: "O, woe is me / T' have seen what I have seen, see what I see!" (163–64). These must be among the most moving lines of the play, especially in the way that Ophelia sets herself up as a spectator and audience of the tragedy. We can only sympathize with her experience of loss, disintegration, and deliquescence. Nothing remains fixed. The highly formal, poetic language of this soliloquy is unusual in its attempt to establish personal loss. Through their common sorrow, Ophelia is made to sound like Hecuba and the Player Queen.

Hamlet's odd soliloquy at the end of the Play Scene, "'Tis now the very witching time of night" (3.2.396) – what I have been calling the "Now could I drink hot blood" (398) soliloquy – has been discussed in some detail in Chapter 6. In its vaunting resolve to be cruel but not to commit matricide, it is very different from the other soliloquies of the play. Hamlet is closest to the heroic mode of Norse mythology in this soliloquy, which also ends with a resounding couplet declaration of purpose:

> How in my words somever she [his mother] be shent,
> To give them seals never, my soul, consent!
>
> (3.2.406–7)

The Prayer Scene with Claudius intervenes between Hamlet's determination to test and punish his mother and his arrival at her closet. On the way, he passes through the King's closet, or private, withdrawing room, and finds him at prayer. Hamlet's presence here is both accidental and incidental, so that his encounter with Claudius at prayer can hardly be the great opportunity that he either misses or refuses. Like the earlier juxtaposition in III,i of Claudius' aside and Hamlet's soliloquy, the Prayer Scene sets the soliloquies of Claudius and Hamlet against each other. It looks, formally, as if Hamlet's soliloquy is inserted into Claudius' soliloquy, which concludes with a neat couplet after Hamlet's exit: "My words fly up, my thoughts remain below. / Words without thoughts never to heaven go" (3.3.97–98).

These soliloquies turn on misperceptions and dramatic ironies. Although he is standing right there, Hamlet by convention cannot overhear what Claudius is saying. Shakespeare avoids any awkwardness by having Hamlet enter at line 72 when the king is kneeling and trying to pray. Claudius is conveniently unaware of Hamlet's presence. There is an air of magic and mystification in the scene, since we in the audience are well aware of everything that is going on. Hamlet honestly believes that Claudius is praying, just as he believed that Ophelia was busy with her orisons in III,i. The characters are required to trust the visual indicators of prayer unless they prove to be suspect. There are certain fixed rules in highly conventional stage situations, so that there is no way for Hamlet to break into the audience's awareness.

Hamlet is remarkably jaunty and colloquial in his soliloquy, as he enters on his way to his mother's closet with sword in hand. He feels that now, after the triumph of the *Mousetrap* play, the initiative is his and he can afford to be on the offensive. All of this bravado, of course, ends with the slaying of Polonius, but for the

moment Hamlet can indulge himself in a swaggering style: "Up,
sword, and know thou a more horrid hent" (3.3.88). He can
luxuriate in perfect scenarios for revenge:

> When he is drunk asleep, or in his rage,
> Or in th' incestuous pleasures of his bed,
> At game a-swearing, or about some act
> That has no relish of salvation in't . . . .
>   (3.3.89–92)

Claudius' final couplet soliloquy dashes all of Hamlet's fantasies:
"My words fly up, my thoughts remain below. / Words without
thoughts never to heaven go" (97–98). Hamlet's assumptions have
been totally wrong: Claudius has not been praying at all, just as
Ophelia's prayer is only a "color." And Claudius, too, has been
spared the sight of the demonic avenger with sword in hand
hovering over him. Nothing can shake the King's complacency
and self-satisfaction, especially not the truth that the audience
knows through dramatic irony. Claudius is already sufficiently
aware that his attempt at prayer is mere "shuffling" (61), but he
cannot muster any real penitence or contrition.

  The King's soliloquy at the end of Act IV, Scene iii presents us
with another expository bombshell when we learn that he is
sending Hamlet to instant death in England. We need to know
more about Claudius the murderer and how he operates,
something we have only heard about in the Ghost's narration in
Act I, Scene v. We will be further enlightened by the triple plot
the king concocts with Laertes against Hamlet in Act IV, Scene
vii. The Claudius of this soliloquy is a terrifying figure, racked
with anxiety and impatience, and the soliloquy itself has an
impetuousness and desperation we see nowhere else in the play:

>   Do it, England,
>   For like the hectic in my blood he rages,
>   And thou must cure me.   (4.3.65–67)

The soliloquy demonstrates the "sickly days" (3.3.96) Hamlet
predicted for his uncle at the end of the Prayer Scene. In his final

couplet, Claudius anticipates the urgency Macbeth shows to get rid of Banquo and Macduff:

> Till I know 'tis done,
> Howe'er my haps, my joys were ne'er begun.
> (4.3.67–68)

The King cannot rest easy and enjoy the fruits of his first murder until Hamlet is disposed of. Soliloquy allows Claudius full scope for his breathless malice. There is no need to equivocate or palliate his homicidal intent as there would be in the social, public, dialogue form. It is important to think of this soliloquy in relation to the more sympathetic soliloquy of the Prayer Scene. In both there is a deadly clarity of purpose and style.

We have already discussed Hamlet's final soliloquy, "How all occasions do inform against me" (4.4.32) in Chapter 6. The speech is very precisely prepared when Fortinbras's Captain exits and Hamlet gets Rosencrantz out of the way: "I'll be with you straight. Go a little before" (31). The soliloquy itself is in some ways remarkably unrelated to the immediate context of Hamlet the prisoner being shipped to certain death in England. "How all occasions do inform against me" is the most markedly thematic and sermonistic speech in the play, very close to a prepared oration on the nature of revenge and the dangers of delay. Its fortissimo couplet-ending makes Hamlet's long exit from the play at this point seem like a grand finale:

> O, from this time forth,
> My thoughts be bloody, or be nothing worth!
> (4.4.65–66)

So saying, Hamlet the Exhorter disappears and the homicidal mood of the middle of the play fades away without having had any lasting effects.

III

Offstage speech in *Hamlet* is related to asides and soliloquies in the sense that it stands apart from regular dialogue. The stage situation makes us aware of dimensions of reality beyond, behind, above, and below the stage itself, as if there were a world elsewhere pressing for recognition. The Ghost of Hamlet's father crying in the cellarage beneath the stage is certainly a portentous effect that, in other plays, is rendered by music. In the symbolic scene of the soldiers in *Antony and Cleopatra*, *"Music of the hautboys is under the stage"* (4.3.11 s.d.), and in *Macbeth* we hear *"Hautboys"* from offstage – most probably from under the stage – as the Witches' cauldron sinks (4.1.106 s.d.). In *Hamlet* the Ghost is a semi-comic "old mole," "A worthy pioner," or digger, who is praised for being able to "work i' th' earth so fast" (1.5.162–63). The *"Ghost cries under the stage"* (148 s.d.) with great portentousness: "Swear" (149). This injunction from beyond the grave is repeated three more times: "Swear" (155), "Swear by his sword" (161), "Swear" (181). The Ghost's insistence is attributed to a "perturbèd spirit" (182) to whom the ceremony is extremely important and who cannot rest quietly without it. In this climactic scene of revelations, we are forced to listen to voices beyond and beneath the stage, as if the stage itself were inadequate to circumscribe all of reality.

In the Closet Scene, we hear Hamlet crying from offstage before he enters: "Mother, Mother, Mother!" (3.4.6). These lines are from the Folio and Quarto 1 (only two "mothers" there); they do not appear in Quarto 2. Jenkins omits them from the Arden edition as "a fairly obvious stage accretion,"[6] a point discussed more fully in Chapter 4. Hamlet's offstage exclamations, with all of their slangy overtones in contemporary American speech, prepare us wonderfully well for the mood and tone of the Closet Scene. They are in the spirit of the soliloquy at the end of III,ii: "Let me be cruel, not unnatural; / I will speak daggers to her, but use none" (403–4). Speaking daggers sounds like a stage direction for intoning "Mother, Mother, Mother!" with pain, anger, and sorrow. It is passionate and wrenching and hardly dispensable as a "stage accretion," whatever that may be. We don't know how these lines got into the Folio text, which shows signs of revision from the earlier Quarto 2 text. If they are an actor's interpolation, we are fortunate that so effective a detail has been preserved in the Folio. Presumably someone must have thought it a valuable addition to the Quarto 2 version. Perhaps the offstage cries were revived from an earlier stage version recorded in Quarto 1.

"Mother, Mother, Mother!" is analogous in function to two other offstage exclamations in the Folio text, both of which have been more or less omitted from the Arden edition. In Act I, Scene v, Horatio and Marcellus, who have been avidly seeking Hamlet, call him from offstage (or *"within"*): "My lord, my lord!" (1.5.113). They then appear and find Hamlet, who is still reeling with excitement at the Ghost's revelations. Calling a character from offstage is hardly a portentous matter, but it serves to extend the limits of the stage action and suggest a larger dimension. In IV,ii, several anonymous Gentlemen call Hamlet from offstage (*"within"*): "Hamlet! Lord Hamlet!" (2). Their shouting immediately precedes the entry of Rosencrantz and Guildenstern, who, at this point in the action, have abandoned all pretense of friendship and politeness. They are now strictly police officers of the King. This deterioration of Hamlet's status after the murder of Polonius is obviously reflected in the tone in which the anonymous Gentlemen address Hamlet. Like "Mother, Mother, Mother!" "Hamlet! Lord Hamlet!" is an acted line with its own spoken intensity.

In the Closet Scene, we have to remember that Polonius speaks from behind the arras where he is concealed, which functions as another offstage area. Like any offstage speech, Polonius' cries from behind the arras would necessarily be muffled or otherwise distorted by distance and physical obstacles. Polonius responds gallantly to the Queen's terror at Hamlet's forcing her to "sit down. You shall not budge" (3.4.19). The Queen feels helpless and genuinely threatened: "What wilt thou do? Thou wilt not murder me? / Help, ho!" (22–23). It is at this point that the hapless Polonius cries from behind, "What, ho! Help!" (24), and Hamlet runs him through immediately. His last comment, helpful for the exposition, is: "O, I am slain!" (26). Both Polonius and the Queen correctly interpret the homicidal mood of Hamlet, who has already been arming himself against matricide.

There is one further example of offstage speech, the stage direction in both Quarto 2 and Folio for the entrance of the mad

Ophelia: "*A noise within*: '*Let her come in*'" (4.5.152 s.d.). The "*noise within*" that preludes Ophelia's entrance may include some generalized offstage shouting, but it obviously also focuses on the imperative demand: "*Let her come in*." This is like the various imperatives shouted by the mob in *Julius Caesar*. The mob in *Hamlet* is associated almost exclusively with Laertes and his successful rebellion against the throne of Denmark. In that scene, too, there is "*A noise within*" (4.5.108 s.d.) which announces Laertes' disorderly rabble breaking into the royal presence.

The implications for staging of the asides, soliloquies, and offstage speech in *Hamlet* are rich and various. We cannot simply attribute what happens to staging conventions; we must also study these non-dialogic resources in their immediate context and stage situation. I have already written about that highly expressive play we may call "*Hamlet* Without Words,"[7] which represents a substratum of nonverbal theatrical expression. But the verbal-nonverbal distinction is artificial and does not do justice to our experience in the theater, when we are hardly conscious whether points are made in language, gesture, stage business, or spectacle. The fact that we can postulate a *Hamlet* without words suggests that a good deal of the spoken play lies outside the confines of dramatic dialogue. There are other ways for the language to move. The asides, soliloquies, and offstage speech seem to constitute an internal play, but this is also the wrong image, since even in Hamlet's "To be, or not to be" soliloquy, Ophelia is clearly visible on stage and Polonius and Claudius are not very far away behind the arras. This is hardly private, and there is no reason to consider the privatization of the play a theatrical virtue.

Shakespeare has gone to a lot of trouble to intertwine Claudius' confessional soliloquy in the Prayer Scene with Hamlet's incestuous and murderous fantasies of revenge. The two are counterpointed against each other and cannot properly be interpreted alone. The stage situation of asides, soliloquies, and offstage speech establishes a context within which interpretation must function. None of the great speeches can be disembodied or thought of as private meditations. They all serve the needs of the play, which are sometimes surprising. In the confessional asides of

Claudius, Gertrude, and Laertes, there is an expository intent that seems to speak for the play and to override the immediate expressive requirements of the characters. The fact that even these well-worn dramatic devices and conventions can surprise us is a tribute to the resilience of the play.

9

The imagery of skin disease and sealing

Among the most distinctive imageries in *Hamlet* are those of skin disease and sealing. Why these themes should occur so significantly in this play is a matter for speculation, but both have a special relation to *Hamlet*. By repetition, they tend to force themselves on our attention and emerge as symbolic preoccupations of the play. They seed the mind and make a strong unconscious impression on readers and audiences alike. They are part of the fictions of the play and they function as almost autonomous symbolic systems.

Skin disease in *Hamlet* tends to emphasize hidden and secret maladies, especially of an ulcerative nature. A typical image is of an imposthume, defined by the *Oxford English Dictionary* as "A purulent swelling or cyst in any part of the body; an abscess." Hamlet is disturbed by the pointlessness of Fortinbras's expedition against Poland:

> This is th' imposthume of much wealth and peace,
> That inward breaks, and shows no cause without
> Why the man dies.   (4.4.27–29)

Cotgrave in his French-English Dictionary of 1611 says that an "imposthume" is an inward swelling full of corrupt matter,[1] and it has a clear relation to the something that is rotten in Denmark. A cyst or abscess is basically an inner infection that shows only partially on the outer skin, like the King's fistula in *All's Well that Ends Well* that he "languishes of" (1.1.33–34).

Another crucial image in this theme occurs in the Closet Scene, where the relentless Hamlet refuses to give his mother any false comfort:

> Lay not that flattering unction to your soul,
> That not your trespass but my madness speaks.
> It will but skin and film the ulcerous place
> Whiles rank corruption, mining all within,
> Infects unseen.   (3.4.146–50)

The image of ulceration is alarmingly specific, and the skinning and filming of the sore place is a representation of false appearances: the smooth surface belies the "rank corruption, mining all within" that destroys without being seen. Claudius' secret murder of his brother is the prototype of what "Infects unseen," and allies *Hamlet* with the curse on Thebes in Sophocles' *Oedipus*. Gertrude may be innocent of complicity in her husband's murder, but she is a typically complacent adulteress who looks aside like Jocasta and doesn't want to hear about the "rank corruption, mining all within." The Ghost makes it clear that its "seeming-virtuous queen" was won to Claudius' "shameful lust" (1.5.45–46) before the murder.

The Ghost's narration in Act I, Scene v puts a revolting emphasis on images of skin disease caused by the poison itself, which is described as a "leperous distillment" (64):

> And a most instant tetter barked about
> Most lazarlike with vile and loathsome crust
> All my smooth body.   (1.5.71–73)

The dominant image is of leprosy itself, which renders the Ghost's beautiful, smooth body rough, crusted, and bark-like. The *OED* defines "tetter" as "A general name for any pustular herpiform eruption of the skin, as eczema, herpes, impetigo, ringworm, etc." In *Troilus and Cressida*, Thersites wishes on Patroclus, among other diseases, "bladders full of imposthume, sciaticas, lime-kilns i' the palm, incurable bone-ache, and the riveled fee-simple of the tetter" (5.1.21–23), and Coriolanus curses the tribunes with another powerful tetter image:

> so shall my lungs
> Coin words till their decay against those measles,

Which we disdain should tetter us, yet sought
The very way to catch them.
(Coriolanus 3.1.77–80)

"Measles" was a word confused with "mesel" or leprous in
Shakespeare's time. We remember that the advent of the Ghost
"bodes some strange eruption to our state" (1.1.69), in Horatio's
words. In Shakespeare's time "eruption" was already being used
in the modern dermatological sense for the breaking out of a rash
or pimples on the skin. An eruption of the state is a skin disease of
the body politic.

The preoccupation with skin disease in *Hamlet* is not a random
event but is closely related to the secret murder of Hamlet's father,
who was poisoned while "Sleeping within my orchard, / My
custom always of the afternoon" (1.5.59–60). Claudius is the secret
poisoner, who slips quite naturally into the imagery of concealment, and especially the image of a hideous disease that must be
kept hidden. Immediately after the murder of Polonius, Claudius
inveighs against Hamlet's "liberty," which "is full of threats to
all" (4.1.14). Out of love for Hamlet,

> We would not understand what was most fit,
> But, like the owner of a foul disease,
> To keep it from divulging, let it feed
> Even on the pith of life.   (4.1.20–23)

"Foul" connotes foul smelling and stinking. Although this image is
not specifically one of skin disease, yet it suggests a foul disease like
leprosy.

To Hamlet, his mother's infidelity

> takes off the rose
> From the fair forehead of an innocent love,
> And sets a blister there . . . .(3.4.43–45)

"Blister" is a strong word, equivalent to pustule or ulcer, and it
serves to mark Gertrude as a whore branded in the forehead. It is
curious how strongly evil is represented in *Hamlet* in images of skin
disease, as if Shakespeare were drawing on the Platonic doctrine of
the smooth and beautiful body corrupted at the outermost

integument. The skin is, psychoanalytically, the stimulus barrier between ourselves and the outside world. One of the Clown-gravedigger's complaints about this present age is that "we have many pocky corses nowadays that will scarce hold the laying in" (5.1.166–68). "Pocky" means infected with pox, or syphilis. A tanner's body, however, will last for nine years because "his hide is so tanned with his trade that 'a will keep out water a great while" (5.1.171–72). Why is Hamlet so concerned with how long a corpse may remain in the earth before it rots? To the Clown-gravedigger it all seems to depend on the quality of your skin.

Hamlet thinks of social distinctions in terms of skin and skin disease. For the past three years he has noted that "the age is grown so picked that the toe of the peasant comes so near the heel of the courtier he galls his kibe" (5.1.142–44). Note that it is the courtier who has the kibe, or chapped, ulcerated chilblain on the heel. This is odd in relation to the social hierarchy because one would expect the peasant to have the kibe.

A few additional images of skin disease confirm the strong emphasis on ulceration. When Claudius reaches the climax of his persuasion of Laertes to the triple plot against Hamlet, he says:

> But to the quick of th' ulcer –
> Hamlet comes back; what would you undertake
> To show yourself in deed your father's son
> More than in words?   (4.7.123–26)

"The quick of th' ulcer" means something like "the heart of the matter," but the image is painfully physiological. The "quick" of the ulcer is the most painful place, where the ulcer is only "skinned and filmed," as Hamlet says in the Closet Scene (3.4.148). It is the part most vulnerable to pricking, and Claudius is already expressing himself in terms of his plot: the unbated foil piercing the quick of the ulcer that is Hamlet's life. Near the end of the play, Hamlet is amply justified in speaking of his murderous uncle as "this canker of our nature" (5.2.69). The *OED* defines "canker" as "an eating, spreading sore or ulcer; a gangrene," and the word was used as an equivalent of "cancer" until the eighteenth century.

Images of skin disease dominate *Hamlet* and create a feeling of ulceration, leprosy, and cancer, all of which must be artfully concealed beneath smiling public appearances. The secret murder of Hamlet's father is represented as a dermatological event. We have an uneasy symbolic sense of something rotten in the body politic of Denmark, and the events of the play seem to be occurring symbolically within this diseased body of the state. How can Hamlet lance the purulent ulcer? By the tainting of revenge he becomes part of the disease he sets out to eradicate. In a revenge play there are no pure spirits who can remain aloof from the action in which they are involved.

The imagery of seals and sealing is more innocuous than that of skin disease, yet it figures importantly in the play because it concerns the will and its authentication. As the Clown-gravedigger argues with mock-scholasticism: "an act hath three branches – it is to act, to do, to perform" (5.1.11–12). The seal gives an official shape and sanction to acts. To put one's seal on a document is a deliberate, considered, legally binding act. Sealing has to do with choices and confirmations by which the sealer will be afterwards bound, and it therefore limits infinite possibility to specific finite acts. With eleven examples, *Hamlet* has the most extensive imagery of seals and sealing in Shakespeare. In the nine examples from *The Merchant of Venice*, many are from the sealing of Shylock's bond, and in *Henry VIII* more than half of the eight examples occur in Act III, Scene ii, where Cardinal Wolsey is forced to give up the "great seal." But in *Hamlet* the examples are more various and metaphoric and not so specifically related to what happens on stage.

The literal reference is to a seal as a special, personal sign, usually one's coat of arms, which is impressed upon warmed sealing wax and attached to a document in order to make it legal. It is like a signature, and the two were often used together, as in the legal formula "signed and sealed." Perhaps because the red and pliant sealing wax suggested lips, the most frequent image of sealing in Shakespeare is a kiss, a much repeated commonplace of Renaissance poetry. Venus' inflamed love plea to Adonis turns on the conceit of sealing:

"Pure lips, sweet seals in my soft lips imprinted,
What bargains may I make, still to be sealing?
To sell myself I can be well contented,
So thou wilt buy, and pay, and use good dealing;
    Which purchase if thou make, for fear of slips
    Set thy seal manual on my wax-red lips."
                              (*Venus and Adonis* 511–16)

The imagery is commercial, and Venus seems to be asking for
amorous seals to the bill of sale. "Seal manual," on the analogy of
"sign manual," is a formal way of saying signature. In *The Two
Gentlemen of Verona*, Julia will "seal the bargain" with Proteus
"with a holy kiss" (2.2.7), and Romeo to the seemingly dead Juliet
will "seal with a righteous kiss / A dateless bargain to engrossing
death!" (*Romeo and Juliet* 5.3.114–15). These examples combine the
erotic and the commercial in an odd way, but they give a good idea
of the most familiar connotations of sealing.

   The stage property documents of *Hamlet* would have conspicuous
seals to show that they were properly executed and therefore
authentic. About Claudius' "grand commission" (5.2.18) to
England ordering the death of Hamlet, we learn that "everything
is sealed and done" (4.3.56), and Hamlet has already told his
mother:

        There's letters sealed, and my two schoolfellows,
        Whom I will trust as I will adders fanged,
        They bear the mandate . . . .   (3.4.203–5)

Since the placing of a seal on a document was the final act that
completed it and made it valid – an important consideration in the
promulgation of edicts and decrees – the image came to indicate an
irrevocable finality. With Claudius' sealing of Hamlet's death
warrant goes a sense that this is as binding as fate; we would say
that Hamlet's doom is sealed. To seal a document or letter meant,
by the way, only to impress one's seal upon it, but the practice was
to close it up with wax fixed in position with one's seal. Anyone,
then, could easily tell if the wax had been tampered with. Through
a confusion of homonyms, "seal" was considered an equivalent of

"seel," meaning to stitch up the eyelids of a hawk (or other bird) as part of its training, so that the two words both came to be used for closing or shutting.

In the final scene of the play, Hamlet has escaped from Claudius' lethal mandate, and, with a mischievous burlesque of court etiquette, he gives Horatio the details of his only partly miraculous salvation:

> making so bold,
> My fears forgetting manners, to unseal
> Their grand commission . . . .   (5.2.16–18)

"Unseal" is the word in Folio, whereas Quarto 2 reads "unfold." The grand commission would be opened by removing the seals that held it closed, but it would also have large and official seals at the bottom, presumably after the signature. With the resourcefulness of the picaresque hero, Hamlet "Devised a new commission" (32) in his best court hand, which now did him "yeomen's service" (36) – good, efficient, useful service, the first recorded use in English of this familiar phrase.

The practical Horatio immediately gets to the greatest difficulty of all: "How was this sealed?" (47). All of Hamlet's brilliant forgery, with parodic flourishes, would be useless if heaven did not show itself "ordinant" (48):

> I had my father's signet in my purse,
> Which was the model of that Danish seal,
> Folded the writ up in the form of th' other,
> Subscribed it, gave't th' impression, placed it safely,
> The changeling never known.   (5.2.49–53)

Notice that Hamlet gives the writ the impression of the sealing wax with his father's signet after he has folded it up. A "signet" is a small seal, usually carved in intaglio in a finger ring, and this is why a signet ring is so often used as a mark of personal identity. In *King Lear*, Kent in disguise dispatches a Gentleman to Cordelia with his ring: "show her this ring, / And she will tell you who that fellow is / That yet you do not know" (3.1.47–49), and in *Richard II* York sends a servingman to his sister-in-law Gloucester with only a ring to authenticate the errand: "Bid her send me presently a thousand pound. / Hold, take my ring" (2.2.91–92).

Hamlet describes every step in his devising the new commission in great detail and with elaborate ceremony. The new document is folded in the proper way, signed ("Subscribed"), given "th' impression" of old Hamlet's signet, then returned to Rosencrantz and Guildenstern's "packet." The incident is a crucial proof to Hamlet of God's providence. The "rashness" (5.2.7) he speaks about is a way of engaging in direct action without the diabolic premeditation of "deep plots" (9). Hamlet has acted with a boldness and a sureness in this matter we have never seen before, and the unexpected signet of his father confirms the truth of the Ghost in a splendidly practical way. The inspiration of Hamlet's escape sets the tone for the fencing match, in which he defies "augury" and trusts instead in the "special providence in the fall of a sparrow" (220–21).

Other documents mentioned in the play are the "sealed compact / Well ratified by law and heraldry" (1.1.86–87) that old Hamlet and old Fortinbras draw up before they engage in their chivalric single combat. Presumably they both set their seals to what seems to be a kind of contract. After Claudius has convinced Laertes of his innocence in Polonius' death, Act IV, Scene vii opens *in medias res* with a request for sealing: "Now must your conscience my acquittance seal, / And you must put me in your heart for friend" (4.7.1–2). An "acquittance" was an actual legal paper or receipt that discharged a person from a debt, on which the careful Claudius is asking Laertes to set his seal to authenticate it. It is a formal request to be released from complicity in Polonius' death. Hamlet's "quietus" that a troubled soul may "make / With a bare bodkin" (3.1.75–76) is an exact synonym of "acquittance."

When it is not used for kisses, the image of sealing most often indicates a decision or choice that has been made, and which is now authenticated by a seal. Our notaries sign documents and affix their seal for purposes of witnessing and attesting, as sealed weights and measures are vouched for by the state. We remember Christopher Sly's "seal'd quarts" in the Induction to *The Taming of the Shrew* (ii, 86). The most complex image of this sort in *Hamlet* is

Polonius' permission for his son's return to France:

> He hath, my lord, wrung from me my slow leave
> By laborsome petition, and at last
> Upon his will I sealed my hard consent.
>
> (1.2.58–60)

No doting old counselor could construct such an elaborate play on words. "His will" is, of course, Laertes' volition or wish, but it is also visualized as a testament on which his father is impressing his seal in the hardening wax. There is some sly play on Laertes' will in contrast with Polonius', whose contents will remain a dark secret. After the outrageous punning on "will" in Sonnets 135 and 136, including Will as Shakespeare's first name, these puns seem mild and unforced. The King caps it all when he tells Laertes: "Time be thine, / And thy best graces spend it at thy will" (1.2.62–63), with a probable stress on the second "thy."

Another image that equates seals with acts or deeds occurs in Hamlet's preparation for the Closet Scene:

> I will speak daggers to her, but use none.
> My tongue and soul in this be hypocrites:
> How in my words somever she be shent,
> To give them seals never, my soul, consent!
>
> (3.2.404–7)

A document without seals would be merely words without any active validity, and Hamlet is nerving himself not to be carried beyond words with his mother. The image itself aptly considers sealing as the method of translating desire into volition. The separation between the tongue and the soul is a form of hypocrisy in which words become autonomous. Nothing can actually happen without the will sealing its desire.

We have seen in a number of examples how the will expresses itself in finite acts by a metaphoric process of sealing. As J. V. Cunningham tells us, "the metaphor of sealing derives from the common Aristotelian and scholastic figure of imposing a seal on wax, which represents the relationship of form and matter: the choice of means gives determinate form to the end desired . . . ."[2]

Thus Hamlet speaks of his friendship for Horatio as a decision that he has made after much reflection and which he has formally recorded by sealing:

> Since my dear soul was mistress of her choice
> And could of men distinguish her election,
> S' hath sealed thee for herself . . . .(3.2.65–67)

This is "sealed" in the sense of ratified or confirmed, as Hamlet's "election" in its narrower political sense later "lights / On Fortinbras" (5.2.356–57). In this context of friendship, sealing is extremely formal and legalistic. It is like Hamlet's insistence that Horatio and Marcellus go through a formal ceremony of swearing on his sword after he has listened to the Ghost's narration. He doesn't really need to confirm their secrecy by oath.

When Hamlet evokes the memory of his father in the Closet Scene, his mythological qualities only strengthen the fact that he is also the apotheosis of a man:

> A combination and a form indeed
> Where every god did seem to set his seal
> To give the world assurance of a man.
>
> (3.4.61–63)

"Seal" is used here to mean a cachet of excellence, attested by "every god," as a king's seal would carry the authority and prestige of the sovereign. This passage gives special significance to Hamlet's earlier exchange with Horatio:

> HORATIO. I saw him once. 'A was a goodly king.
> HAMLET. 'A was a man, take him for all in all,
> I shall not look upon his like again.
>
> (1.2.186–88)

To be a man upon whom "every god did seem to set his seal" is imagined to be superior to merely being a "goodly king." Both passages echo the climax of Antony's funeral oration for Brutus:

> His life was gentle, and the elements
> So mixed in him that Nature might stand up
> And say to all the world, "This was a man!"
>
> (*Julius Caesar* 5.5.73–75)

To be a man among men is the ultimate superlative.

There is a bewildering variety of images of seals and sealing in *Hamlet*, which is surprising because the image is so formal and so legalistic. But Hamlet himself is often conservatively ceremonious. He appreciates a Dido and Aeneas play that "pleased not the million; 'twas caviary to the general" (2.2.446–47), and, unlike Polonius, he does not follow popular taste: "He's for a jig or a tale of bawdry, or he sleeps" (2.2.511–12). Sealing is the opposite of impulsiveness, and we see Hamlet throughout the play struggling to contain his passion. The will must be reined in, action must be the product of reflection, and desire must be authenticated by sealing. All of this implies a psychological stance of testing reality and taking formal decisions on which you can set your seal. The imagery of skin disease and the imagery of sealing have this in common: both are set against illusory and false appearances, and both insist on probing the sore place and confirming the truth before taking action. Shakespeare's preoccupation with these two imageries in *Hamlet* is a way of expressing the concerns of Hamlet and other characters. The central issue is one of openness and authenticity, and the play defines what it means to be a man on whom "every god did seem to set his seal."

10

Hamlet as comedy

Hamlet as comedy is an essential aspect of *Hamlet* as tragedy; you can't have one without the other. The comedy defines the tragedy and makes it convincing and poignant. To put it in another way, the comedy is in equilibrium with the tragedy. This doesn't mean that *Hamlet* is a tragicomedy, which is an entirely different genre with a different history. A tragicomedy is a tragedy with a happy ending or a comedy that successfully exploits tragic materials for a comic purpose. *Hamlet* is not that kind of play at all. Rather, it is a special kind of tragedy that needs comedy to extend its range and to define its profound relation to a world of ordinary, believable experience. Comedy needs to establish this world in order for us to feel how profoundly tragedy will violate it.

"Shakespeare's genius lay for Comedy and Humour. In Tragedy he appears quite out of his Element," says Thomas Rymer in *A Short View of Tragedy* in 1693,[1] and we remember that this is the same Thomas Rymer who speaks so cleverly about Desdemona's handkerchief and who believes that *Othello* "may be a warning to all good wives that they look well to their linen." Whether or not we agree with Rymer, we do know that of Shakespeare's 38 plays only 11 can be classified as tragedies, although some of the histories, like *Richard III* and *Richard II*, are tragic in feeling. At any count, however, not more than a third of Shakespeare's plays are tragedies. Comedy figures much more importantly in Shakespeare's tragedies than tragedy does in Shakespeare's comedies. Did he have a natural genius for comedy rather than tragedy? The question is unanswerable, but all of the tragedies have abundant comic, satiric, and grotesque episodes and scenes, and great tragedies like *King Lear* are steeped in comedy. It is part of their basic conception. This is the theme of Susan Snyder's *The Comic Matrix of Shakespeare's Tragedies* (1979), from which I have garnered both encouragement and enlightenment.

Hamlet is a special case because the play is so strikingly unpredictable and adventurous; it is Shakespeare's most original tragedy. Although embedded in popular conventions of the revenge play, *Hamlet* has many anomalous features drawn from philosophy, Norse mythology, satire, and literary and theatrical parody. *Hamlet* is a heady and exciting play like nothing written before it, not even the hypothetical *Ur-Hamlet* on which it is supposedly based. *Hamlet* is unexpected and passionate, a collage of many different kinds of plays, so that it shouldn't surprise us that it is not an unmixed tragedy. Hamlet himself is trying to put together a world that has suddenly fallen apart: "this most excellent canopy, the air, look you, this brave o'erhanging firmament, this majestical roof fretted with golden fire: why, it appeareth nothing to me but a foul and pestilent congregation of vapors" (2.2.307–11). Comedy is needed in *Hamlet* to make the tragedy more poignant and more human. It functions as a reference point for all that will necessarily be deteriorated, destroyed, or made to disappear. Comedy represents the ordinary world we have lost.

If the concept of comic relief has any validity, then the relief comes at moments of the highest pressure and crisis not only to distract our attention from what is going on, but also to return us to the crisis with greater intensity and relentlessness. This is certainly true of all the macabre jesting in the graveyard in *Hamlet* that directly precedes the catastrophe. It is almost unbearable to have jesting and death back to back; the foolish, foppish Osric is the go-between for the deadly fencing match. Shakespeare need not have managed these strange and ironic juxtapositions this way. They might have been played straight, but the grotesque comedy intensifies the tragic effect. We know almost too much about death and dying by the time Hamlet, Claudius, Gertrude, and Laertes go to their doom.

There is a grim sense of tragic relief, too, since Hamlet has finally taken his long-awaited revenge. Whatever was rotten in the state of Denmark has been lanced by the frightening blood-bath with which the play ends. As Fortinbras testifies, Hamlet "was likely, had he been put on, / To have proved most royal" (5.2.398–99). The new regime of Fortinbras will be less royal, but Claudius and everything he represents has been destroyed. Our relief for that resolution is tempered by disappointment that Hamlet's young life should be so tragically wasted. The Ghost of Hamlet has been most thoroughly revenged. Justice has been restored, but, according to the inexorable laws of revenge, the innocent and the guilty are both equally tainted and must fall together. The revenge is triumphant and tragic at the same time.

Comedy and tragedy in *Hamlet* are impure and mixed genres that function together in ways that are often surprising. It is useless to try to convert the comedy into dark or black comedy in order to make it more respectable in a tragedy. This is a fashionable dodge among critics and directors, but I think it is wrong in its orientation, since the effect of comedy in tragedy depends upon sharp juxtaposition without transition or modulation. One genre is set against the other. I have noted at least six comic elements in *Hamlet*, although I am sure there are many more: comic irrelevance, comic satire, comic madness, comic aggression, comic exuberance and wish-fulfillment, and comic mastery of anxiety. There is a certain overlapping of these six aspects, and many of the examples can easily be made to fit into several categories. The point is that one item cannot be isolated from another. Taken together, the comedy in *Hamlet* shapes the play into a special kind of tragedy, which does not fulfill the criteria of Aristotle's *Poetics* nor of the neo-classical Italian commentaries on Aristotle.

I

Comic irrelevance has always been a staple of the clowns in Shakespeare. Launce's long dialogue (or soliloquy) with his dog in *The Two Gentlemen of Verona* (IV,iv) is a brilliant sample of meandering discourse, as is Mistress Quickly's citation of Falstaff in *Henry IV, Part Two* (II,i). There is a glorious and dreamlike moment when it doesn't matter what is said – it can be the most pointless nonsense – but the relaxed and easy mood is inimitable and the time and space are filled with endless talk. The irrelevance creates its own autonomous comic world. This is one of Hamlet's major irritations in his advice to the Players:

> And let those that play your clowns speak no more than is set down for them, for there be of them that will themselves laugh, to set on some quantity of barren spectators to laugh too, though in the meantime some necessary question of the play be then to be considered. That's villainous and shows a most pitiful ambition in the fool that uses it.   (3.2.40–47)

Hamlet is a champion of the author's text, which should not be adulterated by ad-libbing and improvisation. Was Shakespeare the theater-man also such a literalist? We shouldn't take Hamlet's speech as the playwright's statement to the world, since Hamlet in the advice to the Players sounds more like Ben Jonson than Shakespeare.

In the First (or "Bad") Quarto version of *Hamlet*, our hero gives us some samples of what he most despises, tag-lines from forgotten Elizabethan jokes like: "Cannot you stay till I eat my porridge? and, you owe me / A quarter's wages, and, my coat wants a cullison [=heraldic badge], / And, your beer is sour."[2] Why these particular snappers should bring down the house, and thereby interrupt some necessary question of the play, is now obscure to us. We need to reinvent the jokes to which they might have served as punch-lines or tag-lines. It is clear that Shakespeare, as principal sharer in the Lord Chamberlain's Men (later the King's Men), fears the comic irrelevance of his clowns, who had the capacity to ad-lib so successfully that the play would be stopped dead in its tracks. Hamlet represents himself to the Players as an enemy of popular taste. He wants the First Player to deliver a speech from a play that "pleased not the million; 'twas caviary to the general," a play that has no "sallets," or spiciness, "in the lines to make the matter savory" (2.2.446–47, 453). Is Hamlet a snob? He clearly sets his taste in plays against that of Polonius, who's "for a jig or a tale of bawdry, or he sleeps" (511–12). Polonius is the proverbial tired businessman, about whom Broadway producers have their most titillating nightmares.

Polonius, of course, is the great master of comic irrelevance, and he sets the tone for virtually all of the comedy in the play. In *Hamlet* as comedy Polonius is the leading character. He takes over this role from Claudius in *Hamlet* as tragedy, because the King must be rigorously excluded from the comic action. Polonius therefore functions as a Claudius surrogate. Instead of having Hamlet directly confront his uncle, Shakespeare deflects "the pass and fell incensèd points / Of mighty opposites" (5.2.61–62) onto figures who represent Claudius and the present regime in Denmark: most notably Polonius, but also Rosencrantz and Guildenstern and Osric. Hamlet plays out a whole series of wit combats with these figures, all of which he wins. But Claudius is thereby shielded from the comic action, in which he remains menacingly in the background.

Polonius is the heavy, blocking father of comedy, the foolish and self-important old pantalone of the *commedia dell'arte*, who must be shown up, mocked, and converted in order for the young lovers to triumph. One can imagine an entirely different scenario for *Hamlet* in which the hero, after overcoming many obstacles, finally marries Ophelia with her father's and her brother's blessing. That is not in the cards in Shakespeare's play, but the comic potentialities are there to be frustrated. As surrogate father and potential father-in-law, Polonius looms large in Hamlet's imagination. Otherwise, why is it so necessary for Hamlet to bait the old counselor and to triumph over him? Why is Hamlet so preoccupied with Polonius? He traditionally represents all the old-fashioned values that stand in the way of young love. Ophelia is a political and commercial pawn who must "tender" herself "more dearly" (1.3.107) and set her "entreatments at a higher rate" (122) or else she will "tender" her dear old papa "a fool" (109), which either means that she will make a fool of him or else present him with an illegitimate child. Polonius withdraws Ophelia from Hamlet as the first step in a complex negotiation that may well lead to Ophelia's upwardly mobile marriage to him. Who knows what Polonius may have in mind? He is so devious as not to be fully aware himself where his "windlasses" and "assays of bias" (2.1.65) may lead.

Act II, Scene i shows us Polonius strangely lost in comic irrelevance. His elaborate instructions to Reynaldo on how to spy on Laertes in Paris leave us breathless with confusion. "By indirections find directions out" (2.1.66), but Polonius gets knotted up in his own tedious specifications:

> And then, sir, does 'a this – 'a does –
> What was I about to say? By the mass, I was about
> to say something! Where did I leave? (2.1.49–51)

The wily Reynaldo leads his master a merry chase as he mocks his dotage: "At 'closes in the consequence,' at 'friend or so,' and 'gentleman' " (52–53). Polonius is the senex, a foolish, garrulous, pointless old man like Nestor in *Troilus and Cressida* – and both figures are menacingly powerful. Here comedy impinges on disturbing political truths. Both in the Greek camp and in the court of Elsinore false values ride high. Polonius represents the benighted, stultifying reality of the new regime in Denmark, a bumbling bureaucrat who nevertheless helped the murderer Claudius to the throne and blocked Hamlet's natural succession. The political realities of Denmark do not make Polonius any less comic, but they give a hard edge to his foolery. Rosencrantz and Guildenstern, Osric, and Polonius must all be recognized as dangerous fools.

II

Our second topic, comic satire, pervades not only *Hamlet* but other plays like *Troilus and Cressida* written around the turn of the seventeenth century. Hamlet is a malcontent, melancholy satirist throughout the play because his world has become "an unweeded garden / That grows to seed. Things rank and gross in nature / Possess it merely" (1.2.135–37). Satire is as much a defense against the decay and corruption of the world as it is an expression of disillusion and soured idealism. The death of Hamlet's father and his mother's "o'erhasty" marriage (2.2.57) have embittered the youthful Hamlet even before his encounter with the Ghost. "The funeral baked meats / Did coldly furnish forth the marriage tables" (1.2.180–81) – an example of the cynical "thrift" that now prevails in the new regime. Hamlet must hold his tongue but cannot, so that satire is a natural vehicle for his exasperation with things as they are. Thus the "To be, or not to be" soliloquy catalogues "The slings and arrows of outrageous fortune" (3.1.58) that confront the just man in his daily life:

> Th' oppressor's wrong, the proud man's contumely,
> The pangs of despised love, the law's delay,
> The insolence of office, and the spurns
> That patient merit of th' unworthy takes . . . .
>   (3.1.71–74)

These suggest not great moral affronts but the petty, insufferable irritations of a mean-spirited bureaucracy.

Hamlet's satirical energies turn most easily to woman's frailty, and he unleashes on Ophelia all the bitter jibes meant for his mother. Like Adam's Eve, Ophelia is a painted woman trying to ensnare mankind: "I have heard of your paintings, well enough. God hath given you one face, and you make yourselves another. You jig and amble, and you lisp; you nickname God's creatures and make your wantonness your ignorance" (3.1.144–48). Hamlet is preoccupied with the standard topics of anti-feminine satire, so that his description bears little relation to the Ophelia we see on stage. Hamlet's imagination has converted her into the Whore of Babylon who must stand in for all of womankind. In the Play Scene, he lashes out against the defenceless Ophelia with only slightly veiled innuendos: "That's a fair thought to lie between maids' legs" (3.2.121–22), all the while insisting archly that he doesn't mean "country matters" (119). He is as obviously preoccupied with "country matters" as Alexander Portnoy. Ophelia can only protest weakly: "You are merry, my lord" (125) – "merry" in the sense of sportive and lewd.

In the Closet Scene Hamlet pursues his mother with even more deliberate satirical violence, as he conjures up the primal scene in all of its lurid histrionics:

> Let the bloat King tempt you again to bed,
> Pinch wanton on your cheek, call you his mouse,
> And let him, for a pair of reechy kisses,
> Or paddling in your neck with his damned fingers,
> Make you to ravel all this matter out . . . .
>   (3.4.183–87)

This is hardly satire in its normative, reformational sense, since Hamlet seems to wallow in the very "rank sweat" of his mother and uncle's "enseamèd bed, / Stewed in corruption, honeying and making love / Over the nasty sty –" (94–96). This is self-indulgent rather than cathartic, and it is obviously not meant to be translated into the stage action. Hamlet is the satirist as soloist, enjoying every moment of his inflamed diatribe.

The satiric portraits in the Graveyard Scene are more what we expect from satire, and they have more relevance to an indictment of the society of Claudius' Denmark. As the gravedigger turns up skulls, Hamlet identifies them: "This might be the pate of a politician, which this ass now o'erreaches, one that would circumvent God" (5.1.79–81). Circumventing God recalls the "shuffling" of Claudius' attempt at prayer (3.3.61). The sycophantic courtier who comes next "might be my Lord Such-a-one, that praised my Lord Such-a-one's horse when 'a went to beg it" (5.1.85–86). These are all court figures, including "my Lady Worm" (89). Hamlet is preaching his comic sermon on vanity.

The lawyer is the most extended study in vanity:

> Where be his quiddities now, his quillities, his cases, his tenures, and his tricks? Why does he suffer this mad knave now to knock him about the sconce with a dirty shovel, and will not tell him of his action of battery?   (5.1.100–4)

Not being operative, the lawyer can no longer take an action of battery against the gravedigger. Hamlet delights in his mastery of legal jargon, which can no longer protect the dead lawyer against the live gravedigger. It is only "Words, words, words" (2.2.194). The lawyer is transformed into "a great buyer of land, with his statutes, his recognizances, his fines, his double vouchers, his recoveries" (5.1.105–7). Osric, too, is a rich landowner, "spacious in the possession of dirt" (5.2.89–90), and we remember that Shakespeare himself was a great buyer of land, with most of his theatrical earnings invested in real estate in Stratford and environs. He must have known at first hand the technical vocabulary of notaries and scriveners if he bothered to read the legal documents that he signed. This is the final, *memento mori* irony:

> Is this the fine of his fines, and the recovery of his recoveries, to have his fine pate full of fine dirt? Will his vouchers vouch him no more of his purchases, and double ones too, than the length and breadth of a pair of indentures? The very conveyances of his lands will scarcely lie in this box, and must th' inheritor himself have no more, ha? (5.1.107–14)

At the brink of death, Hamlet is trying, through satire, to free himself from all material encumbrances. He is exorcizing the base, money-grubbing world of Claudius and the court of Elsinore, and by so doing is laughing his enemies to scorn. He has only contempt for the world he is leaving, although when he dies he insists that Horatio remain behind to "report me and my cause aright" (5.2.340) and clear his "wounded name" (345).

III

Comic madness, our third topic, has been so much discussed that Hamlet's "antic disposition" has almost been crushed by the weight of the evidence. It is clear from other revenge plays that Hamlet is not literally mad. He resolves "To put an antic disposition on" (1.5.172) as one might put on a costume or take on a particular role. "Put on" implies acting and artifice. Hamlet may be wrought up, frenzied, even hysterical from grief and the pressure of events; he is distracted but not lunatic (as Ophelia definitely becomes lunatic). Madness is, conventionally, a disguise by which the revenger gains time to investigate the murder and to prepare his revenge. The mad revenger is protected by his mad antics from direct prosecution. Whatever Claudius thinks of

Hamlet's antic disposition, he cannot proceed against him until the murder of Polonius. Hamlet's madness is a convenient vehicle for bitter satire. Even after he has killed Polonius, Hamlet can still jest obscenely and pointedly with the King. Polonius is at supper, "not where he eats, but where 'a is eaten. A certain convocation of politic worms are e'en at him" (4.3.19–21). Polonius is in heaven, where the King may send his messenger to seek him, but if he "find him not there, seek him i' th' other place yourself" (34–35). Hamlet uses his madness to play a very biting and topical clown's role. The music-hall or minstrel show routines are permitted only to legitimate performers; if Hamlet weren't playing mad he would not be a performer.

Hamlet's madness begins right after the appearance of the Ghost. His "wild and whirling words" (1.5.133) are an attempt to mystify his friends and to excuse him from telling them anything at all. He speaks only in portentous nonsense: "There's never a villain dwelling in all Denmark / But he's an arrant knave' (123–24). Horatio protests at being bamboozled: "There needs no ghost, my lord, come from the grave / To tell us this" (125–26). Hamlet's first antic note, then, is to be politic with his friends. With the Ghost, too, he adopts a swaggering, jesting tone that has nothing of his former awe and wonder. As the Ghost moves around beneath the stage for the ceremony of swearing, Hamlet cheers him on with mock hilarity: "Well said, old mole! Canst work i' th' earth so fast? / A worthy pioner!" (162–63). Hamlet is not only trying to conquer his own fears, but he is also actively trying out his antic disposition. He likes the freedom of discourse it gives him.

Polonius is convinced that Hamlet is mad for love, as he himself once was: "And truly in my youth I suffered much extremity for love, very near this" (2.2.190–92). We would like to hear more about Polonius as melancholy lover, as we would also like to learn more about his university acting career: "I did enact Julius Caesar. I was killed i' th' Capitol; Brutus killed me" (3.2.105–6). Hamlet cannot resist the obvious wordplay: "It was a brute part of him to kill so capital a calf there" (107–8). We are reminded of Aubrey's apocryphal story that every time Shakespeare's father, who was a whittawer or tanner of white leather, killed a calf, the young

Shakespeare made a speech.[3] Like Hamlet in some ways, Polonius demonstrates great comic versatility: he can be all things to all men. In their wit combats, Polonius tries to ferret out Hamlet's love madness, but Hamlet is too clever for him. His madness is a vehicle for the grossest insults: Polonius is a "fishmonger" (2.2.174), with the implication that he is a pimp (like the word "maquereau," or mackerel, in modern French). Pandering leads by direct association to Ophelia, who may conceive as the sun breeds maggots in a dead dog. Hamlet always has the upper hand in his exchanges with Polonius, who is slow and ponderous in puzzling out Hamlet's witty retorts.

Hamlet manages to slip in a sustained portrait of the senex, or foolish old man, as the text he is reading:

> the satirical rogue says here that old men have gray beards, that their faces are wrinkled, their eyes purging thick amber and plum-tree gum, and that they have a plentiful lack of wit, together with most weak hams. (2.2.198–202)

Polonius accepts all satirical gibes with gracious forbearance, either because he is too stupid to understand their personal thrust or because he wants to humor the mad Hamlet, who is important to his own political career. In his asides, however, he acknowledges that Hamlet's madness is full of insights: "Though this be madness, yet there is method in't" (207–8) and "How pregnant sometimes his replies are! A happiness that often madness hits on, which reason and sanity could not so prosperously be delivered of" (210–13). Just on the point of understanding the creative role of Hamlet's witty madness, Polonius prudently stops short.

With Rosencrantz and Guildenstern, Hamlet plays mad with less conviction and more irony. As they press in on him after the Play Scene and try to pluck out the heart of his mystery, Hamlet turns aggressively mad. He cannot make his mother a wholesome answer because his "wit's diseased" (3.2.328–29), though he can protest that Rosencrantz and Guildenstern are trying to play upon him like a recorder. Later, after the murder of Polonius, the aggression becomes more naked as Hamlet madly strikes out at everything of which the sycophantic pair stand most in awe. "The

King is a thing" (4.2.28) – this is strong, but, luckily, "a knavish speech sleeps in a foolish ear" (23–24). The obtuseness of Rosencrantz and Guildenstern protects them from the dangerous world of wit.

IV

We have already said a good deal in passing about our fourth topic, comic aggression, which is an intrinsic part of all the comedy in the play. Hamlet is trying to defend himself and to strike out against his enemies through wit; as an isolated and mad revenger he is obviously forced to live by his wits. Everything in the play is set against him, so that his mere survival is problematic, not to speak of his revenge. Comic aggression presents a very Hobbesian world, in which laughter is a "sudden glory,"[4] an expression of superiority over your enemies. Hamlet needs to mock the stupidity, crassness, and philistinism of his enemies in order to belittle them. That is why the play is so much preoccupied with style, especially an aggressive style that asserts superiority.

Polonius is mercilessly ridiculed for his bad taste and for his ornamental rhetoric. The passionate speech of the Player about Pyrrhus killing old Priam is "too long" for Polonius, but the much-moved Hamlet has a quick and insulting comeback: "It shall to the barber's, with your beard" (2.2.510). Is "la barbe" an Elizabethan in-word for boredom, as it is in French? Hamlet picks up the antique word "mobled" from the Player's speech as if he didn't understand it: " 'The mobled queen'?" (514), but Polonius rushes in to commend something he knows nothing about: "That's good. 'Mobled queen' is good" (515). He is itching to score a stylistic point against Hamlet. Why should the deadly/playful wit combats between Hamlet and Polonius be so deeply entrenched in matters of style and language? It is obviously a way of displacing the more literal conflict between Hamlet and his enemies.

When Polonius reads aloud Hamlet's love letter, he gets a chance to strike back at what he considers Hamlet's affectedly poetic style: " 'To the celestial, and my soul's idol, the most beautified Ophelia' – That's an ill phrase, a vile phrase; 'beautified' is a vile phrase" (2.2.109–11). "Mobled" is good but "beautified" is vile, and Polonius sets himself up as an arbiter of proper diction and good taste.

Polonius' own style represents the refinements of school rhetoric gone mad, as he twists in and out of meaningless stipulations and specifications, the very "windlasses" and "assays of bias" (2.1.66) of his Machiavellian manner. He imparts the secret cause of Hamlet's madness to the King and Queen in an oration that is both extraordinarily formal and pointless:

> My liege and madam, to expostulate
> What majesty should be, what duty is,
> Why day is day, night night, and time is time,
> Were nothing but to waste night, day, and time.
> Therefore, since brevity is the soul of wit,
> And tediousness the limbs and outward flourishes,
> I will be brief. (2.2.86–92)

With all the good will in the world, the impatient Queen demands "More matter, with less art" (95), and the wily old orator forswears artfulness with characteristic artifice:

> Madam, I swear I use no art at all.
> That he's mad, 'tis true: 'tis true 'tis pity,
> And pity 'tis 'tis true – a foolish figure.
> But farewell it, for I will use no art. (2.2.96–99)

Why is this style so reprehensible? After Hamlet has killed Polonius in the Closet Scene, his most persistent image is that he has finally silenced a tedious old fool, a compulsive talker and an imperturbable bore:

> Indeed, this counselor
> Is now most still, most secret, and most grave,
> Who was in life a foolish prating knave.
> (3.4.214–16)

Hamlet, "The glass of fashion and the mold of form" (3.1.156), cannot abide "the prating knave" who represents everything that is most opposed to civility and gentility. Part of the rottenness in the state of Denmark is the rottenness of discourse, of which Polonius is the leading practitioner.

When Hamlet tangles with Laertes in the open grave of Ophelia, he seems to be most offended by Laertes' insufferable rant. He too is a prater like Polonius, and Hamlet cleverly parodies his bombast:

> And if thou prate of mountains, let them throw
> Millions of acres on us, till our ground,
> Singeing his pate against the burning zone,
> Make Ossa like a wart! Nay, an thou'lt mouth,
> I'll rant as well as thou.   (5.1.282–86)

Laertes' inflated discourse dishonors the memory of Ophelia and her already maimed funeral rites. We remember that Hamlet has also made merciless fun of himself in his soliloquy after the Player's speech for his own exaggerated and pompous declamations. He is an ass because, "like a whore," he unpacks his "heart with words" and falls "a-cursing like a very drab, / A scullion" (as in Folio) (2.2.597–99). It is a fault of style and therefore also a fault of truth and morality.

V

Most of the comedy we have been speaking about in *Hamlet* is extremely purposive and functions in an ongoing debate between true and false values, with the new regime of Claudius being especially vulnerable to comic attack. But there are moments in the play when Hamlet is high-spirited and exuberant without any ulterior purpose. His triumphs are ironically short-lived, yet, as a fifth aspect of comedy, these moments are noteworthy. They fit into an idea of comedy as wish-fulfillment; that is, that comedy projects wishes, even far-fetched and impossible ones, that suddenly come true. This endows the protagonist with a sense of magical control over reality; nothing can go wrong for him.

Hamlet's escape from Claudius' nefarious plan to have him put to instant death in England is such a moment. Its feeling of invulnerability cannot last, and we know that Hamlet's escape from one death plot only lands him in an even more inescapable trap in which he is certain to die. But it doesn't matter because Hamlet feels that the "interim" is his "And a man's life's no more than to say 'one'" (5.2.74). Hamlet experiences providential euphoria just before the catastrophe, as he tells Horatio the details of his escape. It is an exciting narrative:

> Up from my cabin,
> My sea gown scarfed about me, in the dark
> Groped I to find out them, had my desire,
> Fingered their packet, and in fine withdrew
> To mine own room again, making so bold,
> My fears forgetting manners, to unseal
> Their grand commission . . . .   (5.2.12–18)

Hamlet's sense of triumphant fun is nowhere more marked than in this passage, and the whole account is steeped in the language of sexual intrigue: "Groped," "Fingered," "had my desire."

Suddenly, everything is going right for Hamlet. Heaven shows itself "ordinant" even in small details, because Hamlet has in his purse his "father's signet," "Which was the model of that Danish seal" (49–50), so that Hamlet's new commission can be properly sealed and authenticated. The foolish and malicious Guildenstern and Rosencrantz now "go to't" (56), which makes a slangy pun on the pair going to their death in England as well as pursuing it with vigorous, active, competitive energy, as one might encourage runners in a race to "go to't." It would have delighted Hamlet no end to hear the news from the ambassadors to England:

> The ears are senseless that should give us hearing
> To tell him [i.e., Claudius] his commandment is fulfilled,
> That Rosencrantz and Guildenstern are dead.
> Where should we have our thanks?   (5.2.370–73)

If only Hamlet were alive at this moment, he could have answered that question with appropriate hilarity, in the spirit of Stoppard's *Rosencrantz and Guildenstern Are Dead*.

Hamlet is also wonderfully exuberant after his triumph over Claudius in the Play Scene. It doesn't matter that his victory is

meaningless, and that Hamlet, by revealing to Claudius that he
knows too much, can now be safely marked for death. Hamlet
thoroughly enjoys this delicious moment that he has long been
waiting for. Parodying Kyd's *The Spanish Tragedy*, he proclaims his
Mousetrap play a comedy:

> For if the King like not the comedy,
> Why then, belike he likes it not, perdy.
> (3.2.299–300)

The lines in *The Spanish Tragedy* are:

> And if the world like not this tragedy,
> Hard is the hap of old Hieronimo.
> (4.1.197–98)[5]

Hamlet likes his own production so much, especially his "dozen or
sixteen lines" which the Player has set down and inserted (2.2.551–
52) into the *Mousetrap* play, that he now wants to turn professional:
"Would not this, sir, and a forest of feathers – if the rest of my
fortunes turn Turk with me – with two Provincial roses on my
razed shoes, get me a fellowship in a cry of players?" (3.2.281–84).
Horatio grudgingly offers half a share, but the banter flies thick
and fast as Hamlet sings snatches of derogatory ballads about the
imminent downfall of kings.

The entrance of Rosencrantz and Guildenstern immediately
indicates how wrong Hamlet is. But in his buoyant mood Hamlet
cannot resist some obvious jokes. When Guildenstern gravely
reports that the King "is in his retirement marvelous distemp'red,"
Hamlet quips: "With drink, sir?" (307–9), touching on the Danish
national character. Hamlet continues with threatening bravado:
"Your wisdom should show itself more richer to signify this to the
doctor, for for me to put him to his purgation would perhaps
plunge him into more choler" (311–14). Hamlet's comic swagger is
totally lost on the narrow-purposed Rosencrantz and Guildenstern,
who are natural enemies of comedy. Later, after the murder of
Polonius, when the pair are puffed up with a sense of their own
importance, Hamlet knows how to get at their fat-witted, Secret
Police pride in being like an ape's apple, which he keeps "in the

corner of his jaw, first mouthed, to be last swallowed" (4.2.18–19), or like sponges: "it is but squeezing you and, sponge, you shall be dry again" (20–21). Hamlet's exuberant comedy is at its best in these trenchant insults, and the scene ends with Hamlet leading them a merry chase off the stage (at least in the Folio version): "Hide fox, and all after" (30–31). This is the cry of a children's game like hide-and-seek. The cumbersome Rosencrantz and Guildenstern cannot choose but follow; they are not accustomed to disobeying orders, even from their prisoner.

VI

Our final topic – the comic mastery of anxiety – includes all the others, since, as Freud thought, the essential purpose of comedy is to teach us how to live in an irrational and possibly meaningless world. The Graveyard Scene is undoubtedly the great comic scene in *Hamlet*, poised as it is just on the edge of the catastrophe. To classically-minded critics, it has always seemed absurd to bring on the Clown-gravedigger and his assistant for an elaborate series of riddles, jokes, and logic-chopping at what should be the highest moment of excitement in the play. Shakespeare is taking a high risk on this low-comedy scene, which threatens to ruin the tragic effect. But it is energetically successful because it insists so powerfully on talking about death in all of its gruesome physical details. The tragic effect is intensified beyond the narrative of Hamlet and his revenge.

The Clown-gravedigger and his assistant have verbal routines that remind us of Shakespeare's earliest comedies. Most of the humor turns on riddling wordplay. Was Adam the first that ever "bore arms" (5.1.34)? How could Adam, the first man, have had a coat of arms? That's an anachronism, but how could Adam dig without arms? That's a truth right out of Scripture. Shakespeare must have been sensitive on the subject of arms, since, after great efforts on his part, his family was awarded, shortly before the writing of *Hamlet*, a coat of arms with the motto: "Non Sanz Droict," "not without right." Ben Jonson, who was not averse to twitting Shakespeare on his literary and social pretensions, gives the clown Sogliardo in *Every Man Out of his Humour* a crest that reads: "Not without mustard," which is more relevant to the eating of boiled beef than to an ancient and noble lineage.[6]

The riddles of the Clown-gravedigger in *Hamlet* come out of old jokes that everyone in the audience must have known (or thought they knew). "Who builds stronger than a mason, a shipwright, or a carpenter?" (5.1.51–52). Obviously a gravemaker because "The houses he makes lasts till doomsday" (60). Death becomes familiar and domestic in this discourse; it loses its sting. When Hamlet engages the Clown-gravedigger, we seem to be entering on another wit-combat like those with Polonius. But the Clown takes the lead and Hamlet is put on the defensive:

> HAMLET. What man dost thou dig it for?
> CLOWN. For no man, sir.
> HAMLET. What woman then?
> CLOWN. For none neither.
> HAMLET. Who is to be buried in't?
> CLOWN. One that was a woman, sir; but, rest her soul, she's
> dead. (5.1.132–38)

Touché! Hamlet has lost that round, and he acknowledges it with a certain spoilsport chagrin: "How absolute the knave is! We must speak by the card, or equivocation will undo us" (139–40). It is strange that Hamlet protests against the punning, equivocating use of language. He has never before insisted on speaking literally, by the shipman's or mariner's "card," or chart with compass points.

The Clown sets Hamlet up for jokes at his expense, even jokes about himself as "young Hamlet" – "he that is mad, and sent into England" (151). Hamlet as straightman rises to the bait:

> HAMLET. Ay, marry, why was he sent into England?
> CLOWN. Why, because 'a was mad. 'A shall recover his wits
> there; or, if 'a do not, 'tis no great matter there.
> HAMLET. Why?
> CLOWN. 'Twill not be seen in him there. There the men are as
> mad as he. (5.1.152–57)

So the Clown leads Hamlet on, metadramatically, and the

conversation takes a specific turn about how long a man will "lie i' th' earth ere he rot" (165). Why does Hamlet need all this macabre information?

Everything moves inevitably to the identification of Yorick's skull, the official clown at the court of Hamlet's father, "a fellow of infinite jest, of most excellent fancy" (186–87). In an enormous flood of nostalgia for the past as it was before the corrupted regime of King Claudius, Yorick becomes the hero of this scene. Hamlet's questions pierce the tragic mutability of time:

> Where be your gibes now? Your gambols, your songs, your flashes of merriment that were wont to set the table on a roar? Not one now to mock your own grinning? Quite chapfall'n? Now get you to my lady's chamber, and tell her, let her paint an inch thick, to this favor she must come. Make her laugh at that.
> (5.1.191–96)

We are kept aware of the grinning skull that Hamlet holds in his hands, "quite chapfall'n." Death has the last laugh.

Hamlet as comedy doesn't end at this point. We must still face young Osric, the preposterously affected courtier who brings Hamlet the challenge to the fencing match. Why have an invitation so fatal carried by a messenger so ridiculous? That is a typical Shakespearean move, and it offers Hamlet a final opportunity to express his utter contempt for the new style of the new regime. Osric is a "waterfly," a "chough," a "lapwing" who "runs away with the shell on his head" (5.2.187–88). His only redeeming quality is that he is "spacious in the possession of dirt" (89–90) – that is, land – and is therefore someone "the drossy age dotes on" (191). He is so mechanically ceremonious that Hamlet imagines him as a nursing infant who "did comply," or make compliments to and flatter, "his dug before 'a sucked it" (189–90).

Osric inspires Hamlet to exuberant parody of what he has just said in praise of Laertes:

> But, in the verity of extolment, I take him to be a soul of great article, and his infusion of such dearth and rareness as, to make true diction of him, his semblable is his mirror, and who else would trace him, his umbrage, nothing more.   (5.2.116–21)

Hamlet is having great fun with Osric's stilted and excessively polite diction, and so is Horatio. Yet there is something wrong. In a few moments Horatio will say: "You will lose this wager, my lord" (210), and Hamlet will express his own forebodings: "But thou wouldst not think how ill all's here about my heart" (213–14). If the comic banter with Osric bodes ill, then it is also a way for Hamlet to deal with that ill, to make it assailable and to master his anxiety. This makes Hamlet and Horatio's laughter with Osric all the more hearty and therapeutic.

In speaking of *Hamlet* as comedy, it is noteworthy how many important characters are excluded from the comic action: Claudius, Gertrude, Laertes, and Ophelia. Hamlet must grapple with Claudius through his representatives, most notably Polonius, but also Rosencrantz and Guildenstern and Osric, who all function as comic butts. Hamlet's intensely comic concern with Polonius is surprising, but it is not at all surprising that Polonius should be Hamlet's first casualty in the play. This is part of the irony of "purposes mistook" (5.2.385). "Thou wretched, rash, intruding fool, farewell!" says Hamlet, "I took thee for thy better" (3.4.32–33). It is important for Hamlet to defeat Polonius in the comic action in order for him to defeat Claudius in the tragic action; one event seems contingent on the other. But the play does not have the wish-fulfillment symmetry of comedy, and even the extravagant scene with Osric leads directly into the blood-bath of the fencing match.

In the context of Pinter and Beckett, Ionesco, Dürrenmatt, and Stoppard, I think we understand the whole topic of *Hamlet* as comedy differently from the way it was conceived in the earlier twentieth century. Comedy has come to seem more important in its own right without needing tragedy to complete it and validate its meanings. In our time, tragedy is becoming much more difficult to write, if not to understand. The point of *Hamlet* as comedy is already announced in what may be Shakespeare's earliest tragedy, *Titus Andronicus* – an exuberant, energetic, and intensely lyrical play that has been much maligned by critics. After his daughter Lavinia has been ravished and has had her tongue cut out; after his two sons, Martius and Quintus, have been falsely accused and sent off to the slaughter; and after Titus has foolishly sent his own left hand to try to win mercy for his sons, he is at a low point in his emotional resources. His brother Marcus reminds him that "Now is a time to storm; why art thou still?" (3.1.263), but Titus only laughs: "Ha, ha, ha!" (264). In what follows, the values of comedy and tragedy are set strongly against each other:

MARCUS. Why dost thou laugh? It fits not with this hour.
TITUS. Why, I have not another tear to shed.   (3.1.265–66)

Hamlet is not so sentimental as Titus, but right from the beginning of the play he too has "not another tear to shed."

Conclusion

We have tried to follow the windings and turnings of *Hamlet's* fictions through three broad areas: passion as a key word and key concept in all of its varieties of expression; the taming of the dramatic energies into a meaningful narrative; and the stylistic, theatrical, and genre conventions assumed in the play. We have not dealt thoroughly with any of these topics, but we have tried to provide a sampling of the possibilities. The fiction-making in *Hamlet* creates the play, and its vividness and immediacy are a product of our own aroused imaginations. We are asked to believe in what the characters are doing, or at least for the nonce to suspend our disbelief. The Players in Pirandello's *Six Characters* are most insistent and strident in their claims that it is real, that it is really happening. In *Hamlet* we too get caught up in the fiction that what is occurring on stage impinges on us and our consciousness. It cannot be dismissed as something alien and other. This is the black-comedy point of Stoppard's *Rosencrantz and Guildenstern Are Dead*. We feel their terror and entrapment in a play that is patently histrionic.

I have been trying to argue for the excitement and authenticity of *Hamlet* without stumbling on moral and ethical points. Do we believe in the experience of revenge and all the troubling questions it forces us to ask? In this sense *Hamlet* poses the largest questions about murder, retribution, justice, the value of living in an unjust world, adultery, love, politics, and the Danish succession. We follow the fictions of the play with fascination and without any feeling of a satisfactory and final solution. Much depends on our willingness to remain open at the end. After all the deaths, what consolation? The world of Fortinbras and the new regime lack grandeur and nobility. But the smiling villain Claudius is gone and with him everyone else of substance in the play. We are starting anew with fear and trembling. It may be difficult to believe in fictions, even hypothetically and by proxy, but *Hamlet* is startling in its demands on us. We need to recreate the intense pressures of what could happen "But in a fiction, in a dream of passion . . . ."

If we are interested in the stresses, strains, and anxieties in *Hamlet*, what is the relation of the play to Shakespeare? Does it help him to deal with problems relating to the fantasy play world as a reconstructed and compensatory model of the real world? The Player has no trouble firing up his fictive passion for Hecuba, whereas Hamlet seems at a standstill in his own well justified and passionate revenge. The *Mousetrap* play acts out, in a simplified and violent narrative, the story of which Hamlet is a part. It is like a dream in the clarity of its detail. Hamlet's revenge is projected into a variety of powerful histrionic images. There is an easy solution to the infinite regress of dream images in Hamlet's "rashness" in Act V. His escape from certain death in England occurs in a sea voyage that has the fluidity and quickness of a dream – it is only narrated, not shown. By the workings of Providence, everything falls right for Hamlet. The exciting narrative shows us the way out of the impasse imposed by the dream of passion. It is no longer simply a dream of passion; it is now also a passionate dream. Hamlet escapes a fortuitous death only to die more fittingly when he has accomplished his revenge.

Of course, there is no distinction between the play world and the real world in *Hamlet*; it is all part of the same play. Yet Shakespeare manages to convince us of the fictionality of the fall of Troy and Pyrrhus' slaughter of old Priam as well as the far-fetched *Mousetrap* play only by also convincing us of the reality of Hamlet, Elsinore, the Ghost, and the hidden murder. This is a remarkable feat of doubling the perspective. For Shakespeare as for so many other writers, the fiction within the fiction, the play within the play, offers a clue out of the labyrinth. We see everything clearly through Hamlet's eyes, despite (or perhaps because of) his antic disposition. Shakespeare creates a historical world in which he can move comfortably.

The so-called impersonality and anonymity of Shakespeare are relevant here. He was not remembered by his contemporaries in any distinctive way except as "gentle," which doesn't get us very far. Jonson projected himself as a burly, angry man – he was known to have killed a fellow actor, Gabriel Spencer, in a duel. Robert Greene fictionalized his own life (and death) as an exposer of cony-catching enormities. Even in his very brief work, Webster leaves a distinct imprint of flamboyant and violent melancholy. Marston poses as the Timonist malcontent satirist ready to excoriate the world for its follies. Chapman is distinctively difficult and philosophical in his exposition of a new Stoicism. Next to these – and we could continue with other colorful writers of the age – Shakespeare as a personality is strangely unmemorable. He seems to disappear into the diversity of his characters.

This flight from identity is in itself significant. By depriving us of other clues, Shakespeare himself seems to be forcing us to think of him in relation to his works. It is more than coincidental that Hamlet, too, is trying to establish his identity – as son, lover, crown prince, thinker, drama critic, playwright, and revenger. "This is I, / Hamlet the Dane" (5.1.259–60) he asserts in an unguarded moment. His wide diversity of styles (including self-parody) shows him experimenting with roles and identities. But Laertes is always himself, and so are Fortinbras and Horatio. The point of fantasy is that it is multiple and compensatory. Shakespeare could project an almost infinite number of desired selves. Yet always the problem remains of how to actualize and literalize the dream of passion. Obviously someone who was decisive would not need to speculate about the infinite modalities of passion.

If we need to define what is distinctively Shakespearean, we must turn to the plays and poems of Shakespeare rather than to his life. That is undoubtedly the way Shakespeare has chosen to present his personality. There is always great variety and great richness of detail. There is a consistent interest in experimentation, in trying out new personas and new guises. Shakespeare's characters – at least the more interesting ones – tend to be protean.

They cannot be fixed in a single constellation of traits. Even the mooning and love-sick Romeo surprises us at the beginning of the play by falling in love all over again with Juliet, daughter of his family's direct enemy, the Capulets. As Ben Jonson complained so often, Shakespeare threw his lot in with romance, rather than with the stricter, more classical play that Jonson wrote. Romance means a commitment to fictionality, to story, to dream images. Even Shakespeare's only farce in the style of Plautus, *The Comedy of Errors*, is softened by an abundance of romantic detail.

Finally, Shakespeare tried to do justice to the fullness of life. The fiction and the dream of passion may ultimately be more satisfying than finite action. As the Player King in the *Mousetrap* play of *Hamlet* puts it so grandly:

> What to ourselves in passion we propose,
> The passion ending, doth the purpose lose.
> The violence of either grief or joy
> Their own enactures with themselves destroy . . . .
>
> (3.2.200–3)

In the Player King's formulation, passion and purpose are so closely allied that without strong feeling our own "enactures" tend to destroy themselves. To be passionate is to be alive, and that is why the fiction and the dream of passion are essential to survival.

Notes

Introduction

1 William Empson (1953) "*Hamlet* When New," *Sewanee Review*, 61, pp. 15–42, 185–205.

2 See Maurice Charney (1973) "Shakespeare's Unpoetic Poetry," *Studies in English Literature*, 13, pp. 199–207.

3 See Joseph Papp (1969) *William Shakespeare's "Naked" Hamlet*, New York.

4 The ideological and symbolic relation of *Hamlet* to its first audiences is the central theme of Roland Mushat Frye (1984) *The Renaissance Hamlet: Issues and Responses in 1600*, Princeton.

5 Quoted and modernized from E. K. Chambers (1930) *William Shakespeare: A Study of Facts and Problems*, Oxford, I, p. 411.

6 Quoted and modernized from J. S. Farmer (1909–14) *Old English Plays, Student's Facsimile Edition*, London, Vol. 163.

7 L. C. Knights (1961) *An Approach to "Hamlet,"* London, p. 11.

8 L. C. Knights (1947) "Prince Hamlet," in *Explorations*, New York, p. 87.

9 Ibid., p. 83.

10 L. C. Knights (1961) *An Approach to "Hamlet,"* London, p. 81.

11 P. R. Grover (1967) "The Ghost of Dr. Johnson: L. C. Knights and D. A. Traversi on *Hamlet*," *Essays in Criticism*, 17, p. 152.

12 Kenneth Muir (1962) "Recent Studies in Elizabethan and Jacobean Drama," *Studies in English Literature*, 2, p. 249.

13 T. S. Eliot (1932) "Hamlet," in *Selected Essays 1917-1932*, New York, p. 125.

14 Ibid., p. 126

1 Hamlet's dream of passion

1 C. T. Onions (1958) *A Shakespeare Glossary*, 2nd edn, Oxford, p. 158.
2 See Jack J. Jorgens (1977) *Shakespeare on Film*, Bloomington, Indiana, Chapter 15.
3 T. S. Eliot (1932) "Hamlet," in *Selected Essays 1917-1932*, New York, p. 124.
4 Quoted in Maurice Charney (1969) *Style in "Hamlet,"* Princeton, p. xv, from Coleridge's *Table Talk*, June 24, 1827.

2 How Pirandellian is Shakespeare?

1 The September 1981 issue of *Modern Drama*, Vol. 24, has a number of essays on Pirandello and Shakespeare, especially those of Naomi Conn Liebler, Jill L. Levenson, Matthew N. Proser, and myself.
2 The affinities between Pirandello's *Henry IV* and Shakespeare's *Hamlet* have been noted by virtually all critics of Pirandello. See Anne Paolucci (1974) *Pirandello's Theater: The Recovery of the Modern Stage for Dramatic Art*, Carbondale, Illinois, and (1980) "Pirandello and the Waiting Stage of the Absurd (With Some Observations on a New 'Critical Language')," *Modern Drama*, 23, pp. 102–11. See also Roger W. Oliver (1979) *Dreams of Passion: The Theater of Luigi Pirandello*, New York.
3 Luigi Pirandello (1962) *The Rules of the Game*, tr. William Murray, in *To Clothe the Naked and Two Other Plays*, New York, p. 91.
4 Luigi Pirandello (1952) *Six Characters in Search of an Author*, tr. Edward Storer, in *Naked Masks: Five Plays by Luigi Pirandello*, (ed.) Eric Bentley, New York, p. 258.
5 Tom Stoppard (1968) *Rosencrantz and Guildenstern Are Dead*, New York, pp. 33–4.
6 Luigi Pirandello (1974) *On Humor*, translated and edited by Antonio Illiano and Daniel P. Testa, Chapel Hill, North Carolina, p. 113.
7 Quoted in Eric Bentley (1953) *The Playwright as Thinker*, New York, p. 148.

3 Ophelia and other madwomen in Elizabethan plays

1 See J. Leeds Barroll (1974) *Artificial Persons: The Formation of Character in the Tragedies of Shakespeare*, Columbia, South Carolina, especially Chapter 1. See also Winfred Overholser (1959) "Shakespeare's Psychiatry – and After," *Shakespeare Quarterly*, 10, pp. 335–52.

2 See Paolo Valesio (1970–1) "The Language of Madness in the Renaissance," *Yearbook of Italian Studies*, 1, pp. 208ff.

3 (1973) *The Complete Works of Christopher Marlowe*, (ed.) Fredson Bowers, Cambridge, Vol. I.

4 Cited by Valesio, p. 209, n. 23, from Stith Thompson's motif F950.4, "Marvels."

5 John Webster (1964) *The Duchess of Malfi*, (ed.) John Russell Brown, London, The Revels Plays.

6 See Harold Jenkins's British Academy lecture of 1963, (1963) "Hamlet and Ophelia," *Proceedings of the British Academy*, 49, pp. 135–51.

7 (1902) *The Complete Works of John Lyly*, (ed.) R. Warwick Bond, Oxford, Vol. III.

8 See E. R. Leach (1958) "Magical Hair," *Journal of the Royal Anthropological Institute*, 88, pp. 147–64.

9 Quoted from the facsimile of *Hamlet* (n.d.) Quarto 1, in the Shakespeare Quarto Facsimiles series (ed.) W. W. Greg, Number 7, Oxford.

10 See Samuel Schoenbaum (1975) *William Shakespeare: A Documentary Life*, New York, p. 208.

11 John Marston (1965) *Antonio's Revenge*, (ed.) G. K. Hunter, Lincoln, Nebraska, Regents Renaissance Drama series.

12 Thomas Kyd (1959) *The Spanish Tragedy*, (ed.) Philip Edwards, London, The Revels Plays.

13 John Webster (1960) *The White Devil*, (ed.) John Russell Brown, London, The Revels Plays.

14 (1811) *The Dramatic Works of Beaumont and Fletcher*, (ed.) George Colman, London, II, p. 299.

15 Thomas Middleton and William Rowley (1958) *The Changeling*, (ed.) N. W. Bawcutt, London, The Revels Plays.

4 Hamlet's O-groans and textual criticism

1 Quoted from the Norton facsimile edition of the First Folio, (ed.) Charlton Hinman, New York, 1968. This edition uses a system of continuous, through-line numbering.

2 J. Dover Wilson (1934) *The Manuscript of Shakespeare's Hamlet and the Problems of Its Transmission*, Cambridge, I, pp. 77–9.

3 C. J. Sisson (1956) *New Readings in Shakespeare*, London, II, p. 258.

4 Quoted from the Shakespeare Quarto Facsimiles series, Number 1, ed. Sir Walter Greg and Charlton Hinman, Oxford, 1939.

5 Alice Walker (1953) *Textual Problems of the First Folio*, Cambridge, Chapter 6.

6 Quoted from Edwin Nungezer (1929) *A Dictionary of Actors*, Ithaca, New York, p. 74.

7 (1966) *The Dramatic Works in the Beaumont and Fletcher Canon*, (ed.) Fredson Bowers, Cambridge, I, p. 87. *The Knight of the Burning Pestle* is edited by Cyrus Hoy.

8 Thomas Heywood (1961) *A Woman Killed with Kindness*, (ed.) R. W. Van Fossen, London, The Revels Plays.

9 See E. A. J. Honigmann's radical account of the O-groans in (1976) "Re-Enter the Stage Direction: Shakespeare and Some Contemporaries," *Shakespeare Survey*, 29, pp. 117–25. Honigmann argues that the "O's" in dramatic texts are not words but merely "crypto-directions" for the actors to ad-lib. Unfortunately, the author weakens his own authority to speak about stage directions by almost totally ignoring their relation to performance.

10 Thomas Middleton and William Rowley (1958) *The Changeling*, (ed.) N. W. Bawcutt, London, The Revels Plays.

11 Cyril Tourneur (1966) *The Revenger's Tragedy*, (ed.) R. A. Foakes, London, The Revels Plays.

12 John Ford (1966) *'Tis Pity She's a Whore*, (ed.) N. W. Bawcutt, Lincoln, Nebraska, Regents Renaissance Drama series.

13 I am indebted to Lester Beaurline for this link with the Petrarchan and religious traditions. Beaurline notes the *OED* reference (B2) to the *O's of St. Bridget* or *Fifteen O's*, which were "fifteen meditations on the Passion of Christ, composed by St. Bridget, each beginning with *O Jesu*, or a similar invocation." I must acknowledge Professor Beaurline's kindness in reading this chapter and suggesting ways in which the argument could be made more convincing to textual critics. Professor Robert K. Turner, Jr., also contributed to this aim.

14 Harold Jenkins (1960) "Playhouse Interpolations in the Folio Text of *Hamlet*," *Studies in Bibliography*, 13, p. 35.

15 Terence Hawkes " 'That Shakespeherian Rag,' " *Essays and Studies 1977*, (ed.) W. Moelwyn Merchant, London, p. 34. The essay is reprinted, in a revised form, in (1986) *That Shakespeherian Rag: Essays on a Critical Process*, London.

16 Quoted from (1963) *Eighteenth Century Essays on Shakespeare*, (ed.) D. Nichol Smith, 2nd edn, Oxford, p. 55.

17 See Maurice Charney (1973) "Shakespeare's Unpoetic Poetry," *Studies in English Literature*, 13, pp. 199–207.

5 Analogy and infinite regress

1 See André Gide (1948) *Journal 1889-1939*, Paris, p. 41. See also Lucien Dällenbach (1977) *Le Récit Spéculaire: Essai sur la Mise en Abyme*, Paris.

2 See Taylor Stoehr (1966) "Pornography, Masturbation, and the Novel," *Salmagundi*, 2, pp. 28–56.

3 Ibid., p. 56.

4 G. Legman (1975) *Rationale of the Dirty Joke: An Analysis of Sexual Humor*, 2nd series, New York, p. 242.

6 The exact middle of *Hamlet*

1 This is the reading of Quarto; Folio reads: "And do such bitter business as the day . . . ." See the discussion of this point in my *Style in "Hamlet,"* Princeton, 1969, p. 10, n. 6.

2 There is, of course, no definite indication that Hamlet enters the Prayer Scene with his sword drawn. I assume that "Up, sword" (3.3.88) implies that Hamlet must have had his sword out of its scabbard before he can sheathe it.

3 (1968) *Johnson on Shakespeare*, (ed.) Arthur Sherbo, New Haven, II, p. 990 (Vol. VIII of the Yale Edition of the Works of Samuel Johnson).

4 Nero as a classical exemplar of moral anarchy and matricide is a Renaissance commonplace. *The Interlude of Vice (Horestes)* of 1567 has significant Nero references at lines 965 and 1072 (in the Malone Society reprint, (ed.) Daniel Seltzer, 1962), and the Orestes story is generally analogous to that of Hamlet. See Robert S. Knapp (1973) "*Horestes*: The Uses of Revenge," *ELH*, 40, pp. 205–20.

5 See Philip Edwards's New Cambridge edition of *Hamlet* (1985), cited Cambridge, p. 17.

6 This is a problem for those critics who put great emphasis on the theme of delay in *Hamlet*. Someone must have thought that the central passage on delay could be cut without doing significant harm to the play.

7 See S. F. Johnson (1952) "The Regeneration of Hamlet," *Shakespeare Quarterly*, 3, pp. 187–207.

7 Scene rows, broken scenes, and impacted scenes

1 See Emrys Jones (1971) *Scenic Form in Shakespeare*, Oxford, and James E. Hirsh (1981) *The Structure of Shakespearean Scenes*, New Haven.

2 See Maurice Charney (1970) " 'This Mist, My Friend, Is Mystical':

Place and Time in Elizabethan Plays," in *The Rarer Action: Essays in Honor of Francis Fergusson*, (eds) Alan Cheuse and Richard Koffler, New Brunswick, New Jersey, pp. 24–35.

3 See the fascinating discussion of this scene in James L. Calderwood (1983) *To Be and Not to Be: Negation and Metadrama in "Hamlet,"* New York.

8 The stage situation of asides, soliloquies, and offstage speech

1 See the reviews of *Strange Interlude* by Frank Rich and Walter Kerr in *The New York Times* of July 17, 1984 (the London production), February 22, 1985 (the New York production), and March 3, 1985 (a Sunday retrospective by Kerr).

2 Francis Berry (1965) *The Shakespeare Inset: Word and Picture*, London.

3 See Bernard Beckerman (1962) *Shakespeare at the Globe 1599-1609*, New York, p. 186.

4 Quoted from Edwin Nungezer (1929) *A Dictionary of Actors*, Ithaca, New York, p. 74.

5 See J. Dover Wilson (1959) *What Happens in Hamlet*, Cambridge.

6 Harold Jenkins (ed.) (1982) The New Arden edition of *Hamlet*, London, p. 318.

7 Maurice Charney (1965) "*Hamlet* Without Words," *ELH*, 32, 457–77.

9 The imagery of skin disease and sealing

1 Cited from A New Variorum Edition of *Hamlet* (1963) (ed.) Horace Howard Furness, New York, I, p. 324. A reprint of the 1877 edition.

2 J. V. Cunningham (1951) *Woe or Wonder: The Emotional Effect of Shakespearean Tragedy*, Denver, Colorado, p. 29.

10 *Hamlet* as comedy

1 Quoted and modernized from *The Critical Works of Thomas Rymer* (1956) (ed.) Curt A. Zimansky, New Haven, p. 169. See also Susan Snyder (1979) *The Comic Matrix of Shakespeare's Tragedies*, Princeton.

2 See the facsimile of the First Quarto of *Hamlet* in the Shakespeare Quarto Facsimiles series, Number 7, Oxford, n.d., F2^v.

3 See E. K. Chambers (1930) *William Shakespeare: A Study of Facts and Problems*, Oxford, II, pp. 252–3.

4 Quoted from Neil Schaeffer (1981) *The Art of Laughter*, New York, p. 14. The whole passage reads: "Sudden glory is the passion which makes those grimaces called laughter, and is caused by some sudden act of their own that pleases them or by the apprehension of some deformed thing in another, by comparison whereof they suddenly applaud themselves."

5 Thomas Kyd (1959) *The Spanish Tragedy*, (ed.) Philip Edwards, London, The Revels Plays.

6 Ben Jonson *Every Man Out of His Humour*, quoted in Chambers, op. cit., II, pp. 202–3.

Index